M000032254

# TEN
# STEPS

## TO HEAR FROM GOD

CHARISMA
HOUSE

Most CHARISMA HOUSE BOOK GROUP products are available at special quantity discounts for bulk purchase for sales promotions, premiums, fund-raising, and educational needs. For details, write Charisma House Book Group, 600 Rinehart Road, Lake Mary, Florida 32746, or telephone (407) 333-0600.

TEN STEPS TO HEAR FROM GOD
    edited by Charisma House
Published by Charisma House
Charisma Media/Charisma House Book Group
600 Rinehart Road
Lake Mary, Florida 32746
www.charismahouse.com

Unless otherwise noted, all Scripture quotations are taken from the Holy Bible, Modern English Version. Copyright © 2014 by Military Bible Association. Used by permission. All rights reserved.

Scripture quotations marked AMP are taken from the Amplified Bible. Copyright © 2015 by The Lockman Foundation. Used by permission. (www.Lockman.org).

Cover design by Lisa Rae McClure
Design Director: Justin Evans

Visit Charisma House's website at www.charismahouse
.com.

Library of Congress Cataloging-in-Publication Data:
An application to register this book for cataloging has
been submitted to the Library of Congress.
International Standard Book Number: 978-1-62998-663-0
E-book ISBN: 978-1-62998-664-7

16 17 18 19 20 — 987654321
Printed in the United States of America

# CONTENTS

Introduction......................................ix

Chapter 1   Believe God Has a Plan for
            Your Life.......................... 1

Chapter 2   Ask for Directions.................. 12

Chapter 3   Give God a Vocabulary to Speak
            to You............................ 19

Chapter 4   Learn How to Listen................28

Chapter 5   Seek God's Kingdom First..........38

Chapter 6   Surrender Your Will...............51

Chapter 7   Take Action!.....................64

Chapter 8   Consider What Is Already in
            Your Hand........................76

Chapter 9   Don't Lose Focus.................87

Chapter 10  Remember the Why Behind
            the What.........................95

Notes.......................................107

# INTRODUCTION

WHAT IS MY purpose? Does God really have a plan for my life? We've all asked these questions, and sadly many people stumble along, just happening upon the answers. But the Christian life doesn't have to be like a walk in the dark. We can know we are in the center of God's will for our lives. We can know we are walking in our purpose.

This book will not teach you how to reach your dreams or become a star, because in the end none of those things matter at all. This book will help you discover the purpose for your existence. No matter what stage of life or career you are in, the steps revealed in these pages will show you how to discern the voice of God as He speaks to you about your purpose.

If you listen to the feel-good wisdom of the age calling out to you from television and music, magazines and self-help books, you may come to believe that the chief end of being is finding happiness and success in this world. "The sky is the limit," they will tell you. "You can reach the stars and become one yourself." "You can be anything you want to be." "You are the master of your destiny."

But the reality is, how much money you make, whom you know, and the notoriety you receive are very insignificant in and of themselves. One day all the material possessions you have accumulated and fought to obtain will be divided among relatives or sold for pennies at a garage sale. If you're like most people, your name will one day be unknown, and your face will be unrecognizable. Your mortal life force will one day fall away and disappear into an ocean of obscurity. But, my friend, that is not the end of the story. Although our lives will one day come to an end, the kingdom of God will keep moving forward to victory, and herein lies our greatest opportunity. With our mortal hands we can help to build God's eternal kingdom—and that is the greatest privilege any human being could have!

You are not here simply to achieve your own happiness or success. You are here to advance a cause greater than yourself. The ripples your life produces will continue to impact the world for better or worse far beyond your earthly existence, but your life will be only as meaningful as what it propels forward.

On the wall of the south choir aisle of Westminster Abbey hangs a memorial stone to John and Charles Wesley that says, "God buries His workmen, but carries on His work." The Wesley brothers have been dead for many generations, but God's eternal kingdom is still moving forward, and the small part they played in this divine initiative makes their lives valuable and significant.

Before he died, Paul told Timothy, "I am already being poured out as a drink offering, and the time of my departure is at hand" (2 Tim. 4:6, NKJV). Paul saw his life as expendable for the sake of the gospel. He would be poured out like a drink offering and then drop off like exhausted rocket boosters, but not without having done something of eternal importance. With his mortal and finite life he helped to propel God's everlasting kingdom forward. That knowledge brought Paul complete satisfaction.

The reality is that everyone is expending his life and burning through the finite fuel he's been given, yet so many give very little thought to what they are living for. Do you know what you are living for? Do you know what will make your life count? What are you propelling forward with your time, energy, finances, and passion?

God knows exactly what He created you to do. He knows exactly what will give you fulfillment and satisfaction. He has a plan for you, and He knows how to get you there. Let this book help show you the way.

## CHAPTER 1

# BELIEVE GOD HAS A PLAN FOR YOUR LIFE

A N ARTISAN WILL acknowledge that before a masterpiece is ever crafted, it exists in the mind of its creator. Before a brush strokes the canvas, before a chisel touches the stone, before the clay is placed on the potter's wheel, before the artist has anything tangible to display, he first and foremost has a dream. In the artist's mind he already sees what he will create before it exists in the physical world. When the artist Michelangelo looked at a block of cold marble, he saw something others didn't see. He saw a seventeen-foot-tall sculpture that today is known the world over as *David*. Michelangelo saw a masterpiece trapped in that stone, and he worked diligently to set it free.[1]

Our God is much the same way. He is the master artist! While there was still nothing, He saw in His eternal mind every detail of Creation down to the smallest particle. And when it came time to craft mankind, the signature of His creation, He fashioned

Adam with His own hands and breathed into him with His own mouth—and He still does so today. God continues to fashion mankind with His own hands. Psalm 139:13 says, "For You formed my inward parts; You wove me in my mother's womb" (NAS).

Think about that for a minute. The Master of the universe, the eternal, immortal, invisible, all wise God, made you with His own hands. But before He began to weave you together in your mother's womb, He saw you in His eternal mind, down to the smallest detail. And before you were ever born, He had a dream for your life. Perhaps as He was weaving you together in your mother's womb, He said, "I'm going to make this boy into a mighty man of fearless courage!" Or, "I'm going to make this little girl into a mighty prophetess to her generation!" Whatever His dream for your life might be, one thing is for sure: His will for your life is beyond what you could ask or think!

It may seem painfully obvious, but to hear from God about your purpose, you must first believe that you do, indeed, have a purpose. Yet sadly, in classrooms around the world, teachers are indoctrinating impressionable students with the notion that they are an accident, the result of millions of years of random anomalies and lucky deformities, or that what they do with their lives is just a matter of preference and there is no divine designer who created them. But the Bible tells us that God designed us with a purpose in mind. Psalm 139:14 says we have been "made with fear and wonder." It is only in recent years, with advances in science, that we are beginning to understand just how true those words are. Your body is a mind-blowing feat of engineering—an unbelievably complex design.

Consider this: Your body uses more than two hundred muscles just to take a single step.[2] The design of the human eye is so elegant and complex scientists still don't fully understand how it works. It moves on average one hundred thousand separate times in a single day; conducts its own maintenance work while we sleep; has automatic aim, focus, and aperture adjustment; provides color, 3-D images; and can function from almost total darkness to bright light automatically.[3] It can discern more than sixteen million color hues,[4] including seven hundred shades of gray.[5] In fact, Charles Darwin himself said, "To suppose that the eye with all its inimitable contrivances for adjusting the focus to different distances, for admitting different amounts of light, and for the correction of spherical and chromatic aberration, could have been formed by natural selection, seems, I freely confess, absurd in the highest degree."[6]

In one square centimeter of your skin there are

three thousand sensory cells, twelve heat sensors, two hundred pain sensors, seven hundred sweat glands, one yard of blood vessels, three million cells, and four yards of nerves[7] that send messages to our brains at speeds of up to two hundred miles per hour.[8] Your brain weighs only about three pounds yet contains twelve billion cells, each of which is connected to ten thousand other brain cells, making one hundred twenty trillion connections.[9] It generates more electrical impulses in a single day than all of the world's telephones put together[10] yet uses less energy than a refrigerator light.[11]

The DNA molecules in your body contain the most densely packed and elaborately detailed assembly of information in the known universe.[12] Their code is so unbelievably complex that if you printed out all of your body's DNA chemical "letters" in books, it is estimated that it would create enough books to fill the Grand Canyon fifty times![13]

Of course, there is so much more to say about the wonders of gravity and magnetism that science still cannot fully explain, the flawless rhythm of the solar system, the perfect balance of nitrogen and oxygen in the earth's atmosphere that makes life possible, the amazing order in nature that forms a self-supporting system of life, reproduction, and waste disposal. But is any of this necessary? What more evidence do we need that our world has been created with intelligence and purpose than the beauty, order, and design we see around us and within us?

## YOU WERE MADE ON PURPOSE FOR A PURPOSE

No one who has ever been created is an accident, a fluke of nature, the hapless by-product of the union of a man and a woman, or the result of millions of years of unguided mishaps. Every person who has ever been born is a unique creation, an intentional work of art crafted by the hand of the master artist.

God told Jeremiah, "Before I formed you in the womb I knew you; and before you were born I sanctified you, and I ordained you a prophet to the nations" (Jer. 1:5). God both knew and crafted a destiny for Jeremiah the prophet even before his birth. John the Baptist was filled with the Holy Spirit and called to be the forerunner of Jesus even before he was born (Luke 1:15). Samson was called to be a great deliverer before he was conceived in his mother's womb (Judg. 13:4–5).

Isaiah 46:10 says God declares "the end from the beginning, and from ancient times the things that are not yet done." Romans 4:17 says that God "raises

5

the dead, and calls those things that do not exist as though they did." Psalm 139:15–16 says, "You know me inside and out, you know every bone in my body; you know exactly how I was made, bit by bit, how I was sculpted from nothing into something. Like an open book, you watched me grow from conception to birth; all the stages of my life were spread out before you, the days of my life all prepared before I'd even lived one day" (THE MESSAGE).

God called Jeremiah a "prophet" before he was born. God called John a "forerunner" before he was born. God called Samson a "deliverer" before he was born. And He called Gideon "a mighty man of fearless courage" even though he was trembling in a winepress when He found him. God saw inside Gideon the potential He had created in him before he was born. While Gideon was still in his mother's womb, God called him a mighty man of valor, and God never gave up on that dream for Gideon's life.

Before you were even born, before God began to fashion and form you, before He began to knit you together in your mother's womb, He had a dream for you and a plan for your life. He had a holy calling for you to fulfill. Paul told Timothy that it was God "who has saved us and called us with a holy calling, not by our works, but by His own purpose and grace, which was given us in Christ Jesus before the world began" (2 Tim. 1:9).

Gideon was full of imperfections; he was not esteemed highly in the eyes of other people, and he was a downright loser in his own eyes. But God looked at Gideon just as Michelangelo looked at that rejected piece of marble. In Gideon God could see beauty where everyone else saw only defects.

Even if you have been written off by everyone else, even if you think your life is far too flawed to ever be something beautiful, our God is the master artist! He sees a masterpiece in the rock of your life, and He wants to set it free. No matter where you go in life or what you do, whenever God looks at you, He sees inside of you the potential He placed within you, and He is always calling to that potential as He called Lazarus out of the grave, "Come out!" God wants to take your life from the junkyard of the devil and turn it into a masterpiece, a trophy of His amazing grace and mercy.

## GOD'S ANSWER TO YOUR DOUBTS

If you want to hear from God about your purpose, it begins with believing that He has a purpose for you. It's amazing to think that even after the Angel of the

Lord had appeared to Gideon and told him plainly about God's goodwill toward him, Gideon was slow to believe it.

> But Gideon said to him, "Please my lord, if the Lord is with us, then why has all this happened to us? And where are all His wondrous works which our fathers told us about when they said, 'Did not the Lord bring us up from Egypt?' But now the Lord has abandoned us and put us into the hand of Midian." The Lord turned to him and said, "Go in this strength of yours and save Israel from the hand of Midian. Have I not sent you?" But Gideon said to Him, "Please Lord, how am I to rescue Israel? Behold, my family is the least [significant] in Manasseh, and I am the youngest (smallest) in my father's house."
> —Judges 6:13–15, amp

Just as Gideon did, many people struggle with feelings of inferiority. They may have been abused or rejected and as a result have low self-esteem and little self-worth. They may say to themselves, "But I did not come from a wealthy family." "I do not have a good education." "I'm not smart enough." "I was abused." "I do not have any talents or abilities." "I could never succeed."

When Gideon looked in the mirror, all he could see were disadvantages and shortcomings. He doubted that he was capable of greatness and was not convinced the Lord had picked the right man for the job. But the Lord knew exactly what Gideon needed to hear, and He spoke words that went right to the heart of Gideon's inadequacy: "The LORD answered him, 'I will certainly be with you'" (Judg. 6:16, AMP).

These must be the most comforting words in the entire world. To know that God is with you and that He is for you—this is the ultimate assurance. These were the words Gideon needed to hear, and these are also the words you need to hear deep within your spirit as you begin this journey of discovering God's will for your life. Jesus knew you would need to hear them, and this is why He said, "I will never leave you nor forsake you" (Heb. 13:5) and again in Matthew 28:20, "I am with you always, even to the end of the age."

Romans 8:31–32 says, "What then shall we say to these things? If God is for us, who can be against us? He who did not spare His own Son, but delivered Him up for us all, how shall He not with Him also freely give us all things?" God is for you and not against you! Do you need evidence? In this passage of Scripture Paul points to the cross as the ultimate proof of God's goodwill toward us. If God was willing to give His own Son for us, how much more can we trust that He will gladly and generously give us anything and every thing we need?

Do you feel like a failure? Does the past haunt you and define you? Do you have a difficult time believing God is on your side and has your best interests in mind? It's time for you to get a revelation of the goodness of God. He is not looking for perfect people, and He is not intimidated by your past. He desires "to console those who mourn in Zion, to give them beauty for ashes, the oil of joy for mourning, the garment of praise for the spirit of heaviness; that they may be called trees of righteousness, the planting of the LORD, that He may be glorified" (Isa. 61:3, NKJV).

Paul wrote about this same truth in Romans 8:28 when he said, "We know that *all things* work together for *good* to those who love God, to those who are called according to *His purpose*" (emphasis added). When we understand this reality and it becomes part of the fabric of who we are, then we will begin to view every circumstance, both positive and negative, as a situation God can put to work for our good and the furtherance of His purposes. Salvation, atonement, forgiveness, justification, regeneration, redemption, reconciliation—these are all words used to describe what God desires to do in our lives. Turning ashes into beauty is not an auxiliary benefit of the Christian experience; it is the heart of the gospel, and it is God's will for you!

Jeremiah 29:11 says, "For I know the thoughts that I think toward you, says the LORD, thoughts of peace and not of evil, to give you a future and a hope" (NKJV). Does God have a plan for your life? The answer is a resounding yes! But it's even better than that. Not only does God have a plan, but He also has a good plan that is "exceedingly abundantly beyond all that we ask or imagine" (Eph. 3:20). And with that confidence, we can begin our journey, looking "to Jesus, the author and finisher of our faith" (Heb. 12:2), knowing that "He who has begun a good work in you will complete it" (Phil. 1:6, NKJV).

# CHAPTER 2

## ASK FOR DIRECTIONS

THE WORD *SEEK* is an action word. There are some people who say they are seeking God about their purpose, but they are actually just waiting for a "lucky break." A person who is seeking God's will is actively asking for God's direction.

It may seem obvious, but you will never hear from God about your purpose if you don't ask Him what He wants you to do. James 4:2 says, "You do not have, because you do not ask." The importance of prayer may seem like an incredibly simple thing to mention, perhaps an insult to your intelligence. But you would be surprised to learn how many people have simply never taken the time to seriously pray about what God would have them to do. There are times when God will intentionally hold back something He wants to give you simply because you have not stopped to inquire of Him.

Second Chronicles 16:9 says, "For the eyes of the LORD move to and fro throughout the earth so that He may support those whose heart is completely His"

(AMP). This verse is often quoted, but the context of that scripture may surprise you.

In 2 Chronicles 16 Baasha, the king of Israel, was at war with Judah and tried to starve the people out by besieging them at Ramah. So Asa, the king of Judah, "brought out silver and gold from the treasuries of the house of the LORD and from the king's house, and sent them to Ben-hadad king of Aram (Syria)…saying, "Let there be a treaty between you and me…break your treaty with Baasha king of Israel, so that he will withdraw from me" (vv. 2–3, AMP).

Because Asa bought the allegiance of the Syrians with gold from the Lord's house, they rescued the southern kingdom from Baasha. This might seem like a happy ending, but God was not pleased. He wanted to be Judah's defender and deliverer, but Asa looked instead to the Syrians for deliverance. Add to that the fact that he took gold from the Lord's house and gave it to someone else.

Because of this, God sent a prophet named Hanani to King Asa. His message was: "Because you relied on the king of Aram [Syria] and not on the LORD your God, the army of the king of Aram [Syria] has escaped from your hand. Were not the Cushites and Libyans a mighty army with great numbers of chariots and horsemen? Yet when you relied on the LORD, he delivered them into your hand. For the eyes of the LORD range throughout the earth to strengthen those whose hearts are fully committed to him. You have done a foolish thing, and from now on you will be at war" (2 Chron. 16:7–9, NIV).

Fear caused Asa to trust in the king of Syria instead of on the Lord, and this offended God deeply. For this reason God gave Asa over to the very thing he feared most: he was to be at war. Psalm 118:8–9 tells us, "It is better to trust in the LORD than to put confidence in man. It is better to trust in the LORD than to put confidence in princes" (KJV).

So often God stands by ready and willing to help us, but we never ask. We carry unnecessary burdens trying to find a solution to our problems on our own. When we do this, we lose an opportunity to bring God glory—and we lose an opportunity to get the answer we truly need.

Sadly Asa made the same mistake only three verses later: "In the thirty-ninth year of his reign Asa developed a disease in his feet. His disease was severe, yet even in his illness he did not seek the LORD, but [relied only on] the physicians. So Asa slept with his fathers [in death], dying in the forty-first year of his reign" (2 Chron. 16:12–13, AMP).

Repeatedly Asa called for help from foreign armies

instead of from the Lord, and he inherited perpetual war as a result. When he was sick, Asa sought help only from the doctors instead of from the Lord, and he died as a result. God wanted to deliver Asa from his enemies. He wanted to heal him of his illnesses. But as many of us do, Asa didn't turn to God when it mattered most. And the results were disastrous.

The final verse of the chapter sums up Asa's life with an almost contemptuous caption: "They buried him in his own tomb which he had cut out for himself..." (2 Chron. 16:14, AMP). Asa insisted on relying on his flesh rather than God, and the Lord gave him over to what he feared the most. Jeremiah 17:5 says, "Thus says the Lord, 'Cursed is the man who trusts in mankind and makes flesh his strength, and whose heart turns away from the Lord'" (NAS).[1]

If you are seeking God's will for your life, it means that you are actively praying about it, waiting before the Lord, and listening for His direction. Perhaps you have not heard an answer because you haven't asked the question. Perhaps you have asked, but you haven't been listening. Maybe it's time to turn off the television, put away the video games, and spend some time on your knees before the Lord, reading His Word and listening to His voice. His promise is, "You will seek

me and find me when you seek me with all your heart"
(Jer. 29:13, NIV).

## FASTING FOR BREAKTHROUGH

There are times when the answer we seek is delayed.
At times it may even seem as though something is
blocking it. In times like these it may be necessary to
couple our prayers with fasting. In Matthew 17, when
the disciples encountered a demon in a young boy and
could not cure him because of their unbelief, Jesus
told them, "This kind does not go out except by prayer
and fasting" (v. 21). In this passage Jesus was letting
the disciples know that some obstacles are stubborn
and require prayer *and* fasting. For some situations,
there is no other way around.

If you're asking God for direction about your purpose and yet continue to lack clarity, you may want
to consider fasting for a period of time. When we put
our flesh into submission by denying it the things it
desires in pursuit of what God desires for us, our spiritual focus becomes sharper and God responds often in
dynamic ways.

Fasting is uncomfortable, but sometimes you have
to do something unusual, extraordinary, and beyond
the norm to see breakthrough. Normal church, normal

Christianity, normal preaching, and normal praying are not always going to get the job done. When you fast, the authority of God, power of God, and faith of God come alive in you, and you will find yourself getting stronger spiritually.

Throughout Scripture we see the power of prayer and fasting. Esther and the people of Israel went into a three-day fast when they were seeking deliverance from death at the hand of Haman, the king's evil advisor (Esther 4:16). God answered by uncovering Haman's evil scheme. And Daniel fasted for twenty-one days in pursuit of an answer from God. Daniel didn't realize it, but during that time the prince of Persia withstood the answers to Daniel's prayers. His fast helped an angel break through the resistance and bring the answers.

Fasting has the power to bring breakthrough in your life too. Fasting can help break the frustration of unanswered prayer and release divine guidance. It can eliminate confusion, cause clarity, and release understanding and wisdom to make correct decisions. Fasting causes humility, which gets the attention of God, who gives grace to the humble.

Fasting is beneficial whether you fast partially or fully. A partial fast can include some food such as vegetables and can be done for long lengths. Complete fasts consist of only water, and water is important to cleanse the system of toxins that are released through fasting. The Holy Spirit will reveal to you when you need to fast and how long. But if you do not have experience fasting, you may want to begin with a one-day or three-day fast. Total fasts longer than three days should be done by those with experience in fasting or under the clear leading of the Holy Spirit. And while fasting from food is most common, God may direct you to fast from other things, such as television or social media.

However you fast, the purpose is to deny your flesh and feed your spirit. This is why prayer must accompany fasting. Without it, we are missing the whole point of fasting. You may want to spend the time you would be eating in prayer and Bible study.

As you seek to hear from God about His purpose for your life, make a point to ask Him for direction. That may involve fasting for a time, but even if the answer doesn't come right away, don't get discouraged. Remember, the Lord delights in answering our prayers. His ears are open unto the prayers of the righteous (1 Pet. 3:12), and the effectual, fervent prayer of a righteous man avails much (James 5:16). Our God hears prayer, and He wants to answer them. If you will be faithful to seek Him *actively*, He will respond.

## CHAPTER 3

# GIVE GOD A VOCABULARY TO SPEAK TO YOU

THE MOST COMMON way God speaks to us is through His Word. The Scriptures are always speaking to anyone who will take the time to meditate on them.

If you say you desire to hear God's voice yet have no desire to read the Bible, you are fooling yourself. The Scriptures ring with the pitch, the tone, the rhythm, and the meter of God's voice. You will learn to recognize His voice as you cultivate a deep, abiding love for what God has already said in His written Word. God has gone to great lengths to preserve His Word. Many righteous men and women have paid a dear price, even with their blood, so that we could have the Scriptures. If you are not interested enough in what God has already said to take the time to read His Word, then why should He say anything else to you?

An employer sent an e-mail to one of his staffers with detailed instructions on something that needed to be done. The staffer came back to me right away asking for clarification. It was obvious to the employer that he had not taken the time to read the e-mail carefully because in it he had already answered all of the man's questions. Why should the employer repeat all of his instructions just because the staffer didn't take the time to read what he had already said? The employer replied to the questions by simply resending the original e-mail.

Many times we wonder why God doesn't speak to us, but it is so simple: He has already spoken, and we have not taken the time to read what He has said. The answers to many of our questions have been sitting right there in front of us all along gathering dust while we cry out to God for a word from heaven.

If the enemy can keep you from God's Word, he can keep you from God's voice. If you really want to hear from God about your purpose, make time every day to meditate upon the Scriptures. If we learn God's character by reading His Word, we are better able to recognize His voice when He speaks to us personally.

When we spend time in His Word, we get to know His nature and character. And as we discover what He is like, we also learn what He would or would not say. Scripture tells us that:

- God is love (1 John 4:8).

- He is forgiving (Micah 7:18–19).

- He is unchanging (Heb. 13:8).

- He is faithful to keep His promises (2 Pet. 3:9).

- He is good (Ps. 34:8).

- He is kind (Luke 6:35).

- He is merciful (Ps. 136).

- He is full of power (Rom. 13:1).

- He gives us peace that passes all under-standing (Phil. 4:7).

- He is shield to those who take refuge in Him (Prov. 30:5–6).

- He is our provider (Matt. 6:26).

- He desires to give us good gifts (James 1:17).

- He hates sin (Jer. 44:4).

- He expects our obedience (John 14:23).

God has chosen to reveal quite a bit to us about His character and nature through His Word. This gives us a framework to know Him experientially.

To learn God's voice—and His Word—many people choose to memorize Scripture. Developing the habit of memorizing God's Word is most beneficial, because often when God speaks to us, He will bring a particular verse or passage of Scripture to our remembrance. It takes only a few minutes each day to learn one scripture per week. An effective strategy is the "M&M" method, where you *memorize* a scripture for four days and then *meditate* on it for the next three days.

- **Memorize**: You may want to purchase index cards and write the verse on one side and the reference on the back. Then you can study the verses for five minutes per day. Or you may want to put Post-it Notes in the places you frequent—on the bathroom mirror, the refrigerator door, or the dashboard of the car—to memorize Scripture as you go throughout the day.

- **Visualize**: To help make the verse stick, focus on a word picture that might be in

your scripture. Psalm 23 describes green
pastures. How large are they? How tall is
that grass?

- **Emphasize**: Say the scripture out loud
by emphasizing a different word. For
example, Psalm 23:1 would go like this:
  "The LORD is my Shepherd…"
  "The Lord IS my Shepherd…"
  "The Lord is MY Shepherd…"
  "The Lord is my SHEPHERD…"
  Each phrase helps shed a different
perspective and meaning, which will
come as you memorize and visualize
each word.

- **Personalize**: It is a great discovery when
you realize the Bible is God talking to
you personally. Try putting your name
(or a loved one's name) into a scripture. For instance, "No weapon formed
against Michael will prosper" (Isa. 54:17)
or "He who has begun a good work in
Michael will complete it…" (Phil. 1:6).

Be patient as you learn the skill of memorizing
and meditating on God's Word. This process will

become easier the longer you do it. To build a habit of daily Bible study, you may also want to follow a daily reading plan that takes you through the Bible in a year. These are easy to find online and even with your smartphone.

## A WORD IN SEASON

When we know God's Word, the Holy Spirit can bring a scripture to our minds at just the right time so that it provides clear guidance for a present situation. He may use a few verses or whole passage of Scripture to communicate to us, or He may suddenly flood us with scriptures along a given theme. For instance, one time God wanted an evangelist to go on a long fast and pray for her city. In a two-week period she happened upon just about every passage on fasting in the Bible. The verses on fasting seemed practically to jump off the page at her until she finally got the idea that God wanted her to fast and pray for her city.

John 14:26 tells us, "But the Helper, the Holy Spirit, whom the Father will send in My name, He will teach you all things, and bring to your remembrance all things that I said to you" (NKJV). The only way the Holy Spirit can bring something to your remembrance is if it is first in your memory!

## MISUSING GOD'S WORD

As wonderful as the Bible is, it is still possible for believers to misuse it. In her book *How to Hear the Voice of God in a Noisy World* author Teresa Seputis shares two common ways we can misuse God's Word when attempting to hear God's voice: by manipulating Scripture and taking verses out of context.[1] Let's look at each.

### Manipulating Scripture

Many people try to manipulate Scripture to say something God is not saying. Essentially they are putting words in God's mouth. Most people don't do this intentionally, but sometimes we want something so badly we find a scripture to fit our desire then convince ourselves God has promised it to us. The Bible tells us the heart is deceitfully wicked.

As you study Scripture, ask the Holy Spirit to reveal what He wants you to know. Begin your Bible reading by praying, according to Psalm 119:18, "Open my eyes, that I may behold wondrous things from Your law." If you ask the Holy Spirit to illuminate the truth of God's Word to you, He will do so. As a result, you will receive understanding and find great joy in studying God's Word.

## Taking verses out of context

Second, people all too often take God's Word out of context. They use the Bible as a kind of horoscope. They open it each day and think whatever verse they first come across is God's word for them for the day. There may be times when God brings a verse to mind in what seems to be a random way, but that is not His standard way of speaking to us each day through His Word.

There is an old story about a distraught man who decided he would open the Bible in a last-ditch effort to hear from God. His eyes fell upon the words, "And Judas went out and hanged himself." This did not bless him, so he tried it again. His eyes fell on the words, "Go and do likewise." By this time he was nearly at his wit's end, but he tried once more. The verse he got was, "What thou doest, do quickly."

Obviously that wasn't God speaking at all. It is terribly unwise—even dangerous—to "make" the Scriptures tell us what we want to hear.

Satan took Scripture out of context when he tempted Jesus in the wilderness in Luke 4. But Jesus knew God's Word and was able to resist Satan's temptation by putting the Bible back in its proper context. As a result, the Bible says Satan left (v. 13). Because Jesus knew God's Word, Satan was unable to derail God's purpose for His life.

The same is true for us. Learning God's Word gives Him a vocabulary to speak to us, and it gives us a weapon to resist the enemy's attempts to thwart God's plans for our lives. To hear from God about your purpose, develop your knowledge of His Word. Read it, memorize it, meditate on it, and ask God to give you revelation into what you're reading. Knowing God's Word allows you to know God's character, so you will recognize the way He speaks and know what things He would and would not say.

## CHAPTER 4

# LEARN HOW TO LISTEN

THERE IS A small shrub called *dictamnus albus* that grows in Israel (as well as many other places). It is also known as the "gas plant" or "burning bush," because it emits a flammable vapor and has been said to spontaneously combust if it gets hot enough in the desert sun. Some Bible commentators believe the *dictamnus albus* might be the very species of bush Moses encountered.[1]

> The angel of the LORD appeared to him in a flame of fire from the midst of a bush, and he looked, and the bush burned with fire, but the bush was not consumed. So Moses said, "I will now turn aside and see this great sight, why the bush is not burnt." When the LORD saw that he turned aside to see, God called to him from out of the midst of the bush and said, "Moses, Moses." And he said, "Here am I."
> —EXODUS 3:2–4

This is where Moses received his divine call and discovered God's will for his life. But there is an interesting detail recorded here that many people miss. First of all, it's important to note that Moses was not impressed because a bush was on fire. He had lived in the wilderness for forty years. He probably had encountered many *dictamnus albus* bushes before, and perhaps he had even seen them spontaneously combust. But this one was unique because it kept burning and burning and burning, and yet, "The bush was not consumed."

We don't know how long the bush burned before Moses realized something extraordinary was going on. Maybe it burned for a day or a week or a month before he decided to investigate the phenomenon. The Scriptures don't tell us. But one thing is certain. God never shouted out to Moses from the bush, "Hey, you—Moses! Come over here. I have something I want to say to you!" Instead God waited until verse 4. It says when the Lord saw that Moses turned aside to see, then and only then did God call out to him from the midst of the bush.

People often ask, "Why doesn't God speak to me?" Many times the reason is simply because *we aren't listening*! We are often so busy and in such a hurry that we rush right past the Lord and never stop to give Him our attention. Who knows how often we miss an encounter with God or a word from heaven simply because we are too busy to take the time to "turn aside." Some Christians feel very sorry for themselves because it seems they are always being forgotten and passed over. While others have burning bush experiences and receive great revelations from God, they seem to always be left out. They ask, "Is God angry with me? Doesn't He love me? Aren't I special to Him?" My friend, perhaps God has just been waiting for you to slow down and "turn aside."

Once a young Christian told a church deacon he struggled with prayer. The deacon said, "Young man, prayer is easy. It's just talking to God. Talk to Him like you would talk to a friend."

"Yes, I do that," the young man said, "but after about five minutes I've said everything I know to say. Yet I hear other people saying they pray for hours. How can someone pray for so long? What do they talk about?" The deacon began to explain. "First," he said, "you need to make a list of all your friends and relatives on a piece of paper. Then you need to list everything you need from God. Then you need to list everything you can be thankful for…" And the catalog of things to talk with God about went on and on.

As sincere as the deacon was, his advice was terrible. The real secret to prayer is much simpler. In fact, it can be summed up in one word: listen.

Prayer is not about making lengthy lists of requests for God and continually chattering for as long as possible. Sometimes the best thing you can do is to be quiet and listen! Do you think for one second that what you have to say is more important than what God has to say? François Fénelon said, "A humility that is still talkative doesn't run very deep."[2] Learn to become quiet in the presence of the Lord, in a posture of humility and awe, and tune your spiritual ears to His voice. God will speak to you in this place, and you will encounter His presence as Moses did—when you turn aside and listen.

## WHOSE VOICE ARE YOU HEARING?

So what if you are quiet before God? How do you know whether He has, indeed, spoken to you? As we seek to hear from God about our purpose, we must be aware there are also two other voices that may try to get in on the action. When we know how other voices may try to imitate God's voice, it becomes easier to discern when He is speaking.

### God's voice

God's voice is the one we long to hear. God may speak to us directly in what may sound like our own thoughts, or He may use a memory, a verse, or even another person to speak to us. God communicates with us in various ways. But His voice will never contradict His Word or His character. If you can't imagine Jesus doing what you think you're hearing, or if it doesn't reflect the nature of a loving Father, that may very well not be the voice of God you're hearing. The more time you spend with God in prayer, worship, and Bible study, the better you will get to know Him and the easier it will be to know what He is like and what He would say.

**Our own heart**

Sometimes God's voice sounds like our own thoughts, and sometimes what we're hearing is, in fact, our own thoughts. Some people are very critical, and they think they're hearing God say harsh, critical things, but it's their own voice they're hearing. That is not to say the Holy Spirit only gives us nice, rosy messages. It is dangerous to think God will tell us only positive things.

However, God convicts us; He doesn't condemn us (Rom. 8:1). The Holy Spirit's conviction is meant to mature us and change behavior that separates us from Him; condemnation shames us and keeps us immature and feeling hopeless, which pushes us away from God. Conviction empowers, but condemnation prevents us from fulfilling the destiny God has for us.

On the flipside, sometimes our own voice is too lax.

A youth leader shared a story once of two students who she discovered were sleeping together in a hotel. The young man told her with all sincerity, "It was the Lord's idea." His explanation was equally bizarre: "I was sexually active before I gave my life to Jesus, so I know how important it is to be sexually compatible. I really do love her and plan to marry her someday. We even got down on our knees next to that hotel bed and prayed, 'Lord, if you want us to get married, then let our time together be extra special.'"

The error in this young man's thinking is obvious, since God's Word forbids premarital sex. He was hearing the voice of his own desires, not the Lord's. God's voice will never lead us into sin.

**Satan's voice**

The devil can try to imitate God's voice to us. He may quote Scripture to us, as he did to Jesus in the wilderness, but he will twist the meaning in order to lead us astray. Jesus was not taken in by this because He knew the Scriptures and He knew the Father. Believe it or not, you know the Father too. Jesus said, "My sheep hear My voice, and I know them, and they follow Me" (John 10:27). If you are a child of God, you have an inward witness, according to Romans 8:16. That means in your deepest being, you will recognize the things of God.

As God's children we have the Holy Spirit—the Spirit of Truth—residing in us, and Scripture tells us He will guide us into all truth (John 16:13). We can trust God to keep His promise and help us steer clear of the enemy's deception.

## KEYS TO DISCERNING GOD'S VOICE

If there is a question in your mind about whether something you're sensing is from God, ask yourself the following questions.

### Is it biblical?

If the answer to this question is no, then you have your answer. God will never tell you to do anything that is contrary to His Word. Even if what you are sensing feels so real and so strong, watch out! There are many spirits in the world but only one Holy Spirit. And the Holy Spirit will never contradict the Scriptures.

### Is this causing confusion in my heart?

If the answer to this question is yes, then what you are sensing probably is not from God because God is not the author of confusion (1 Cor. 14:33). Jesus likened His people to sheep, and sheep are very easily frightened and confused. God may challenge us to think differently about things or to reach out to new levels of faith, but He doesn't create confusion or the doubt and strife that often accompany it.

## Is this producing peace in my heart?

Jesus's voice comes with an awareness of heavenly peace. In contrast the devil uses urgency, pressure, and fear to drive people. There can certainly be exceptions to this rule. Sometimes the Lord speaks words of correction and rebuke. There are also situations when the word of the Lord is time sensitive and immediate action is required. But most of the time when God speaks, it is not a driving, demanding, high-pressure, "You have to do this right now or else!" word. If you believe God is speaking to warn you of imminent danger and you must react quickly, then do so. But if you believe God is speaking to you to quit your job, sell your house, and go to the mission field before next Thursday, it might be best to slow down a bit, get into the Word, and seek some godly counsel.

## Have I quieted my desires and self-interest?

The voice of our own longings, interests, and opinions can easily be confused with God's voice. To make sure what we are hearing is from God, we must identify our desires and self-interests and, as an intentional act of our will, neutralize them. The louder the voice of our own will, the quieter God's voice will be. Conversely the quieter the voice of our own will, the louder God's voice will be. Therefore, if what you are sensing grows quieter as you silence your desires, then it is not from God. But if what you are sensing grows stronger as you neutralize your own desires, then it just might be from the Holy Spirit.

God loves to speak to people who love Him and desire to live their lives in His presence. He draws near to those who, as an act of their will, have drawn near to Him (James 4:8). The more time we spend alone with Him seeking His face through prayer and worship, the easier it becomes to hear and immediately recognize His voice in our hearts. The greater our love for Him, the more finely tuned our ears will become to hear the sound of His voice.

## YOU ARE ACCOUNTABLE FOR WHAT YOU HEAR

It is wonderful to know God, to be in deep intimacy with Him, and to be able to clearly discern His voice. But as God speaks to you, the more accountable He holds you to obey what He says to you. Jesus tells us over and over that He expects to be obeyed (John 14:15, 21; 15:14). He said in Luke 12:47–48:

That servant who knew his master's will, but did not prepare himself or do according to his will, shall be beaten with many stripes. But he who unknowingly committed acts worthy of punishment shall be beaten with few stripes. For to whom much is given, of him much shall be required. And from him to whom much was entrusted, much will be asked.

These verses tell us that if we want to hear God's voice more clearly, we must fully commit to obeying what He says. This makes sense. Why should He speak to us if we won't obey what He says? If you want to hear God's voice clearly about your purpose, you must commit to obey Him—even if it's uncomfortable. He may ask you to do something you've never done before, such as return to school, share the gospel with a stranger, or step out in faith financially. Make a conscious decision to obey what you hear.

## CHAPTER 5

# SEEK GOD'S KINGDOM FIRST

REDEMPTION HAS BEEN the divine agenda since Adam and Eve fell in the Garden of Eden, and throughout human history God has been working diligently and unrelentingly to this end. Both Old and New Testament scriptures contain hundreds of references that run from start to finish in a seamless thread of single-minded intention.

In fact, according to Acts 3:21 every one of God's holy prophets since the beginning of the world has spoken about the restoration of all things. Those prophecies will be fulfilled, the prayer of Jesus will be answered, and God's kingdom will come. What a day that will be!

This is what we long for. This is what we pray for. This is what we work for—for God's kingdom to come and His will to be done on earth as it is in heaven!

Regardless of what we do as an occupation, we all share a singular calling and mission in this life: to build God's kingdom on earth. This is why our "ship" has been deployed. This is the business we should all be investing in, and if we find ourselves moving in any other direction, we can be sure we are moving away from God's will for our lives.

The building of God's kingdom on earth is not just something we should keep in the back of our minds and try to contribute toward whenever an opportunity presents itself. Seeing God's kingdom come on earth must be our main ambition. In fact, Jesus said, "But seek first the kingdom of God and His righteousness, and all these things shall be *added* to you" (Matt. 6:33, NKJV, emphasis added).

My friend, we have been placed in this world for a purpose: to propel God's kingdom forward. This is more than a preference or privilege; it is a divine responsibility and duty for which we will be held eternally accountable. Propelling God's kingdom forward is not a side issue—it is the reason you were saved, it's the reason you were born. You have come into the kingdom for such a time as this!

## DIVINE ADDITION

Matthew 6:33 says if you will seek the kingdom of God first, "all these things shall be added to you." The Greek word translated *added* is a mathematical term. From a perspective of real value, addition is meaningless unless we are dealing with numbers greater than zero: $0 + 0 = 0$. This is true ad infinitum. One could add zeros together until they stretch around the globe, and still the value of all those added zeros would be zero. Zero is the ultimate value of all the accessories we seek in life. The writer of Ecclesiastes said it best:

> "Meaningless! Meaningless!" says the Teacher. "Utterly meaningless! Everything is meaningless." What do people gain from all their labors at which they toil under the sun? Generations come and generations go, but the earth remains forever. The sun rises and the sun sets, and hurries back to where it rises. The wind blows to the south and turns to the north; round and round it goes, ever returning on its course. All streams flow into the sea, yet the sea is never full. To the place the streams come from, there they return again. All things are wearisome, more than one can say.
>
> —ECCLESIASTES 1:2–8, NIV

The Lord told Isaiah to cry out and to prophesy these words that still ring like an anthem to our world that chases feverishly after possessions, glory, and gratification.

A voice says, "Call out [prophesy]." Then he answered, "What shall I call out? [The voice answered:] All humanity is [as frail as] grass, and all that makes it attractive…is [momentary] like the flower of the field. The grass withers, the flower fades, when the breath of the LORD blows upon it; most certainly [all] the people are [like] grass.…In fact, the nations are like a drop from a bucket, and are regarded as a speck of dust on the scales.…All the nations are as nothing before Him, they are regarded by Him as less than nothing and meaningless.

—ISAIAH 40:6–7, 15, 17, AMP

Movie stars, world leaders, and business tycoons all think they are very important, and nightly news reports would have us believe the world revolves around these people and their influence, power, and wealth. But from God's perspective it is all nothingness and futility. All of their wars, struggles, and efforts to rise to the top of the ladder are all worthless. And if this is so for the most powerful people, how much more for us? When all is said and done, what is the purpose of everything we do? We struggle and toil all our lives, pushing, striving toward something, some purpose, but what?

In an attempt to find meaning, we tell ourselves

that we are doing it all for our children, but what do we teach our children? From us they learn to add zeros together, and thus they inherit the same meaningless futility with which we have lived. All the goods we acquire soon rot, precious moments are forgotten, and money evaporates as the dew. The world keeps spinning and changing as people and kingdoms come and go. The wise will see that "the Teacher" was right—everything in this world is utterly meaningless and has less value than a zero. Yet people spend their entire lives adding these meaningless zeros together.

But when we are seeking first the kingdom of God, it means we have made God's kingdom the priority in our lives. And when God's kingdom is number one, suddenly all the zeros after it have meaning: 10; 100; 1,000; 10,000; 100,000; 1,000,000! All the zeros of life are meaningless unless God's kingdom is first! But put God's kingdom first, and not only will you find ultimate purpose and meaning in life, but also even the small things will take on significance.

The Taylor brothers were both highly ambitious. Both wanted to make a difference. Both wanted their lives to count. The older brother decided to bring honor to the family name by pursuing a prestigious political career. The younger brother decided to dedicate his life to preaching the gospel and went to

China as a missionary. Contemporaries of the Taylor brothers would have certainly seen the older brother as the more successful one, but today he is virtually unknown except for his relation to his younger brother, Hudson.

Hudson Taylor became one of the most well-known pioneer missionaries in history, and he is loved and honored around the world today. One brother sought fame, fortune, and power. His reputation, money, and influence have long since taken flight on the wings of time. The other brother seemed to throw his life away serving God in a distant land. But the legacy of Hudson Taylor lives on because, though he was not a millionaire, a superstar, or a world leader, he gave his little life to something eternal.[1]

The missionary martyr Nate Saint once said, "People who do not know the Lord ask why in the world we waste our lives as missionaries. They forget that they too are expending their lives...and when the bubble has burst, they will have nothing of eternal significance to show for the years they have wasted."[2] Christianity is counter intuitive. It is a paradox and preaches a message that is exactly opposite the world's wisdom. The world says, "Protect your life if you want to save it." Jesus says, "For whoever wishes to save his life will lose it; but whoever loses his life for My sake will find it" (Matt. 16:25, NAS). Solomon, one of the wealthiest and most powerful kings who ever lived, tasted all the world had to offer and came to the conclusion that it is all "meaningless." It is just as the Apostle John wrote, "The world and its desires are passing away, but the one who does the will of God lives forever" (1 John 2:17).

This does not mean you should become a missionary. Not at all. Whenever "God's will" is mentioned, people automatically begin to think of quitting their jobs and going into "the ministry." It is so unfortunate that the body of Christ has often been dismembered by class distinctions between "clergy" and "laity." Those in full-time, occupational ministry have been put on pedestals and are expected to be the ones advancing and representing the kingdom of God while the "normal" Christians are busy with secular enterprises. For many Christians their "faith" is a Sunday morning matter, just one of life's many associations discreetly acknowledged on their personal profile next to political party affiliation and favorite sports teams.

But in Christianity there are no distinctions or classes. We are all a part of the priesthood, and we are all expected to be about kingdom business. God wants your life to be an annexation of His kingdom on the earth! He wants you to be an ambassador for

His kingdom wherever you go and whatever you do. In that sense we are all called to be in "the ministry."

## ALL THESE THINGS

Careers, life partners, finances, location, and education should never be our chief focus. All of these things will be sorted out and added to us as we keep the kingdom of God as our primary concern. As we seek God's will for our lives, we can be sure that it will never move us in a direction that is contrary to God's kingdom purposes.

The imperative of seeking God's kingdom is not only relevant in the context of highly spiritual ministry issues. Jesus says that if we seek the kingdom first, all these things will be added to us. This is one of the most powerful secrets to discovering God's will for your life. If you will set your sights on His kingdom and make that your priority, as you move toward it you will automatically come across everything else you need!

Once after a sermon about the kingdom of God, an elder in the church approached the preacher and said, "You know, all these lofty ideas are wonderful, but most of the people in the church are just trying to figure out how to pay their bills and get along with their spouses and raise their kids and do a good job at work." He was right. Most Christians consider the kingdom of God to be something so lofty that it is best left to pastors and evangelists.

The famous psychologist Abraham Maslow espoused a similar view. He constructed a pyramid that he titled the "Hierarchy of Needs." It was his opinion that before someone could "self-actualize," he first needed to meet the basic needs of human nature such as food, shelter, and companionship. Maslow believed that before one could reach the lofty ideals at the top of the pyramid, he would need to climb from the bottom, meeting the basic needs first.[3] This seems to be the most intuitive approach to life. Many people think the kingdom of God is an ethereal and irrelevant topic, and they prefer to be "down to earth." They have decided to first concentrate on putting food on the table and paying the bills. This seems to be the responsible and practical thing to do.

But what Jesus taught is quite the opposite. Jesus said, "Don't worry about what you will eat or what you will wear. Your Father in heaven knows you need these things, and He will take care of you. Instead seek first the kingdom of God, and all these things will be added to you." (See Matthew 6:25–33.) What Jesus was teaching was Maslow's Hierarchy of Needs in reverse. Jesus turns Maslow's pyramid upside down! Jesus teaches us to start at the pinnacle of the pyramid, the highest and loftiest place. Put the kingdom of God first, and everything else will be taken care of—physical, mental, and emotional needs included.

- If you want to know what job God has for you—seek His kingdom, and you'll find your occupational calling!

- If you want to know whom you should marry—seek His kingdom, and you'll find your spouse!

- If you want to know where you should go to college—seek His kingdom, and you'll land in the right school!

- If you want to know where you should live—seek His kingdom, and He'll lead you to the right geographical location!

Can it really be that simple? Could this one command really be the secret to finding out God's will? My friend, these are not random words. These are not the words of a philosopher or a preacher. These are the words of the Son of God Himself; "But seek first the kingdom of God and His righteousness, and *all these things* shall be added to you" (Matt. 6:33, NKJV, emphasis added).

Many people have put education first in their lives. When all is said and done, they will be highly intelligent fools, missing the greatest wisdom of all in their endless search for knowledge. Many people have put money first in their lives. When all is said and done, they will know the truth of Matthew 6:24: "You cannot serve both God and money" (NIV). Many people put family first in their lives. When all is said and done, it is their family who will pay the price for their misdirected priorities. When we put anything ahead of Christ and His kingdom in our lives, not only will we miss God's kingdom, but we will also miss all the other treasures as well.

## ...BECAUSE WE LOVE THE KING

A word of caution and clarification is due at this point because there are many people who have misconstrued and terribly misunderstood Jesus's promise. They view Christ and His kingdom as a means to an end, a tool to get what they want in life. They have come to Jesus because they see Him as a way to become healthy, wealthy, and wise. They have believed a humanistic version of the gospel that emphasizes the last word of

Matthew 6:33: "All these things shall be added unto *you*" (NKJV). Although there are wonderful fringe benefits to serving God, if those benefits become our motivation, we have missed the point completely.

God is not looking for spiritual "gold diggers" who use Him and His kingdom to get rich, or to become popular or powerful. On the contrary, God is looking for people whose eyes are so fastened on Him and Him alone that none of the peripheral attractions are even in view. It is those with consecrated hearts to whom He says, "Don't worry. I'll take care of everything else you need."

Although seeking God's kingdom first will give us fulfillment and purpose in life, we do not seek God's kingdom primarily for the sake of becoming self-actualized or having a sense of accomplishment. It's true that as we seek God's kingdom, our material and financial needs will be met, but we do not seek God's kingdom primarily because of the monetary benefits. It is obvious that seeking God's kingdom results in eternal rewards that are very literally "out of this world." But we do not seek God's kingdom primarily to win an eternal prize. We do not seek the kingdom because we love its benefits—we seek the kingdom because we love its King! When our love for the King becomes our paramount incentive, then and only then do we have things in the right order.

Building the kingdom of God must be our primary objective in life, but the underlying motivation must be love for the King. The only way a person can be truly committed to the kingdom of God is to be consumed with love for Christ. If we are driven by a philosophy or an ideology, a desire to make the world a better place or to see a new order established, then our ambition falls into the same category as communism, Marxism, socialism, and all the other "-isms." Seeking the kingdom of God is in a category all by itself because it stems from a fountain deeper than any motive in this world—divine, supernatural love for the King. This love is the foundation and the driving force behind the kingdom that will endure long after all others have crumbled to dust.

## CHAPTER 6

# SURRENDER YOUR WILL

IN THE JOURNEY to hear from God about our purpose we must recognize something so simple yet so significant: there may be a difference between what we want and what God wants. With this awareness we must constantly make sure our will is surrendered to His.

Many times people embark on the journey to discover God's will having already made up their minds about what they think God wants them to do. And often what they are actually seeking is divine validation of what they desire. If you truly want God's will for your life, you cannot simply pray, "Your will be done." You must include, "Not my will."

In the Lord's Prayer Jesus said, "Your kingdom come," and with the same breath continued His petition by saying, "Your will be done" (Matt. 6:10). Those phrases may seem to address two completely separate topics, but they actually go hand in hand. In fact, you can't have one without the other.

To understand the correlation between God's

kingdom coming and His will being done, let us first consider what a kingdom is.

In ancient times kings ruled their kingdoms with absolute sovereignty, and their word was law. A kingdom was the realm in which a certain king's authority and will were recognized and obeyed. Let's take a more contemporary kingdom, the British Empire, for example. The American colonies were at one time under the rule of the king of England, and for this reason he was able to collect taxes from the colonists. Even though the king was separated from these American subjects by a great distance geographically, they were a part of his kingdom because they were under his rule. But when the American colonists rebelled and won independence from the empire, they no longer obeyed the wishes of the British king. His will was no longer their concern, because they weren't a part of his kingdom and therefore not under his authority.

There are many people who for some reason think that whenever the Bible talks about the kingdom of God, it is referring to heaven. But when Jesus taught about the kingdom of God, He had something more in mind. If a king's kingdom is the realm in which his will is observed and obeyed, then the kingdom of God is present wherever God's authority is acknowledged and submitted to. Therefore when Jesus prays, "Your kingdom come," He is inferring what He states explicitly in His next breath, "Your will be done."

But the prayer of Jesus is not like Burger King's motto. Jesus isn't saying, "Father, have it Your way as everyone else has it their way." Jesus was praying for God's will to be done exclusively—the way it is done in heaven. In other words, all other wills bow to the divine will, God's authority is recognized and submitted to, and everything comes into alignment with what the Father desires.

## THE KINGDOM "IN EARTH"

The wording of the Lord's Prayer is rendered a bit differently in the King James Version. Jesus prayed, "Thy kingdom come, Thy will be done in earth, as it is in heaven." While some translations say, "Your will be done on the earth," the King James says, "Thy will be done in earth." Genesis 2:7 says, "The LORD God formed man from the dust of the ground." We are made from the earth, we are vessels of "earth," and when God's will is done in us, or "in earth," then and only then can God's will be done "on the earth."

Jesus prayed, "Your kingdom come," and continued by saying, "Your will be done." These are two inseparable conditions. Wherever God's kingdom has come, there His will is being done. Likewise, when God's will is being done, there His kingdom has come. If we are seeking the kingdom first, then the kingdom is our main ambition, and this is demonstrated in two ways. First, we want to see God's will done "in earth" (in our own lives), and second, we seek to see His will done on the earth (in the whole world).

It all begins with the heart—it all begins with us. Many people want to change the world. They want to see the nations bow their knees to the King of kings and the Lord of lords. Yet the hearts and lives of many of these people still aren't surrendered. Jesus said, "The kingdom of God is within you" (Luke 17:21). What was Jesus talking about? He was talking about God's will being done in the hearts of men. Human kings fight over land, but the real estate God desires is that of the heart.

Jesus said in John 7:38, "He who believes in Me, as the Scripture said, 'From his innermost being will flow rivers of living water'" (NAS). He didn't say we would see rivers of water flow from heaven— He said they would flow from inside His people! God's kingdom is not coming out of the blue sky; it's coming from within us! God's will is that every believer becomes an annexation of His kingdom, a portal through which He can pour His glory and release His power into the world. If you want to see God's kingdom come on earth, it starts with God's will being done in earth—in you!

Romans 14:17 says, "For the kingdom of God does not mean eating and drinking, but righteousness and peace and joy in the Holy Spirit." This is the inward condition of people who have submitted themselves to God. They are filled with righteousness, peace, and joy in the Holy Ghost! It's heaven in earth!

## THE BLESSING OF BROKENNESS

"Not My will, but Yours, be done" was not just a prayer Jesus prayed one time before His crucifixion. (See Luke 22:42.) This was the unvarying posture of His heart. He was always living and walking in perfect submission to the will of God. Everywhere Jesus went, He taught about the kingdom, but He didn't just talk about it; He demonstrated it!

First, the kingdom was inside of Him because He was perfectly submitted to His Father's will. And consequently the kingdom was manifest wherever He went: the sick were healed, the dead were raised, and demons fled. "Thy will be done in earth, as it is in heaven" (Matt. 6:10, KJV) was not Jesus's hopeful musing for an imaginary utopia.

Jesus fulfilled His own prayer and showed us how it will be answered. Through Jesus God's will was being done on earth as it is in heaven, and this is what God desires to do through our lives as well. But it all begins when we come to a place where our will is submitted to God's—"Not my will, but Yours, be done." It is in this place of submission that we will discover and fulfill God's will for our lives.

The Greek term translated *seek* is an action word. It is ongoing and continuous. This is important to understand because discovering God's will for our lives is not simply a destination to be reached; it is a posture of the heart! It is not simply a matter of choosing the right career path or marrying the right spouse. It is an ongoing stance of submission to God's will above our own. It is a lifelong prayer, "Not my will, but Yours, be done." As long as we live, we must continue to follow and obey. Discovering God's will for our lives happens daily as we constantly and faithfully seek to know and to do His will.

As we seek God to discover His will for our lives, the narrow road cuts through a dark valley where God tests our hearts and breaks us. The breaking process is uncomfortable but very important to endure if we want to see God's will done in our lives. The valley of brokenness is where we learn to say, "Not my will, but Yours, be done." This brokenness, while painful, releases amazing power and makes us useful to God.

When a cowboy wants to harness the potential of a beautiful and powerful stallion, he sits on the horse's back. This is very uncomfortable to the animal. It has always been its own master. It has always done what it wanted to do. And when the cowboy begins to exert his will over the horse's, a desperate struggle ensues. The horse begins to kick and thrash and buck in an attempt to throw the cowboy off its back. But the trainer will keep getting back on the horse and keep riding it until it stops kicking and bucking. The cowboy knows that until the horse's will is broken, it is of little use. So it is with God's people. Until we are broken, we are of little use to God's kingdom.

In Matthew 14 we read an amazing story about a miracle where Jesus fed a multitude with a just five loaves of bread and two fish. Not only did the meager lunch become enough to feed thousands of people—it became more than enough! After everyone had eaten, there were still twelve baskets full of bread and fish left over! But before the small lunch became a mighty feast, before the little became much, before the miracle of multiplication could take place, it says in verse 19 that Jesus "took the five loaves and the two fish, and looking up toward heaven, He blessed the food, and breaking the loaves He gave them to the disciples, and the disciples gave to the crowds" (NAS). Notice something very important here. It says Jesus did two things: first, He blessed the food, and second, He broke it.

Jesus blesses only what He breaks. God can multiply only what has been broken. Do you want God to take your little life and do something mighty with it? Do you want to be blessed and be a blessing to multitudes? Then you need to be broken.

Verse 20 is careful to specify that the baskets left over were made up of "broken pieces"—"They picked up what was left over of the broken pieces, twelve full baskets" (NAS). At the end of our lives, when all is said and done, and everything has been consumed, the only parts of our lives that will have lasting value are the broken pieces. The way the world looks at things is so different from the way God looks at them. The world values the lofty, powerful, proud, and big. God values a broken and a contrite heart, a heart that is humble and bowed low before the King.

In Isaiah 66:2 the Lord says, "But to this man I will look, even to him who is poor and of a contrite spirit, and trembles at My word." The psalmist says in Psalm 51:17, "The sacrifices of God are a broken spirit; a broken and a contrite heart, O God, You will not despise."

At the Last Supper Jesus took the bread of

Communion and said, "Take and eat. This is My body which is broken for you" (1 Cor. 11:24). This brokenness that He spoke of was the crucifixion He would soon endure. That brokenness would loose the greatest power the world has ever known. The Apostle Paul says, "I have been crucified with Christ. It is no longer I who live, but Christ who lives in me" (Gal. 2:20). When we are crucified with Christ, this death to self is a brokenness that allows the life of Christ to flow out of us. A broken person is a person who is crucified with Christ. It is in this kind of person that God's will is being done and in whom God's kingdom is present and flowing out to the world around him.

## SAY GOOD-BYE TO YOUR VISION

When we talk about being crucified with Christ and dying to self, what do we mean? It means we die to our desires, our ego, and our will. Sometimes this even means dying to our own vision. But you may say, "I'm sure my vision is God-given. It is His will." Yet there is an inherent danger. It is possible for the calling, promises, and vision God has given us to become our main ambition, making them opponents of God, for He is not willing to share our hearts with anything—not even with good things.

Isaac was the fulfillment of the promise God gave Abraham. Yet God was not willing to share Abraham's heart, not even with Isaac. So God asked Abraham to lay Isaac on the altar and offer him as a sacrifice, knowing this would be the ultimate test of Abraham's love. Author A. W. Tozer expounds on this brilliantly in his classic book *The Pursuit of God*.

> God let the suffering old man go through with it up to the point where He knew there would be no retreat, and then forbade him to lay a hand upon the boy. To the wondering patriarch He now says in effect, "It's all right, Abraham. I never intended that you should actually slay the lad. I only wanted to remove him from the temple of your heart that I might reign unchallenged there. I wanted to correct the perversion that existed in your love. Now you may have the boy, sound and well. Take him and go back to your tent. Now I know that thou fearest God, seeing that thou hast not withheld thy son, thine only son, from me."[1]

What does it mean to surrender our will to God? The word *surrender* is a radical word! Many of us are willing to surrender until it begins to hurt, but true surrender is painful. Some people are willing to surrender as long as it is logical, but true surrender is not subject to our rationale. Others can surrender what is bad and harmful, but God is not satisfied. To God surrender is not complete until it is all encompassing, exhaustive, total. It is not simply saying, "Your will be done," but it includes, "Not my will." This death to self is not some form of divine sadism. God always has life in mind. Just as a gardener prunes off the old branches so new ones can grow, God desires to remove that which hinders life and growth. This place of death is also the place of birth, and it is how God's purposes are born in the earth!

John Wimber is best known as the founder of the Vineyard church movement, which is well known for its wonderful music that touched the world and, in many ways, revolutionized worship in the modern church. But many people don't realize that John Wimber had been very successful as a secular musician. Two of his hit singles reached the US top ten before he met the Lord and abandoned fame and fortune to follow Jesus. His wife, Carol, told the following story:

> John and I had been Christians only a few
> months. We were broke and Christmas was
> coming. John had laid down his musical career

because Jesus asked him to. After refusing a lucrative offer to arrange a Christmas album, he quietly put down the phone. As I watched, John went to the cup boards, closets and the piano bench. He gathered a lifetime of work and talent and placed it in big cardboard boxes and we drove to the Yorba Linda dump. As he pushed the last box out of the station wagon and it sunk into the garbage, John 12:24 came to my mind: "Except a grain of wheat fall into the earth and dies, it remains alone, but if it dies, it bears much fruit." In my heart I know that was when worship was born in the Vineyard.[2]

What if God asked you to give up the thing you enjoy the most? What if He asked you to lay down your gift or talent, the thing that defines you—the thing in which you find self-worth? Could you lay your promise on the altar as Abraham did Isaac, or push your treasures into the Dumpster as John Wimber did? Have you checked to see who is sitting on the throne of your heart? Is it you? Is it your vision? Is it your dream? Or is it Jesus?

My friend, God has a wonderful plan for your life, and He wants to use you in extraordinary ways for His glory. But resurrection only follows death—death to self, death to your will, death to your desires, and death to your dreams. It is in these painful moments of surrender that God's kingdom is established in us, when we pray with Jesus, "Not my will, but Yours be done." This beautiful brokenness allows us to become an extension of God's dominion, and our lives become "cracks in the wall" through which His kingdom can come and His will can be done in earth and on earth!

## CHAPTER 7

# TAKE ACTION!

A CERTAIN WELL-KNOWN EVANGELIST was attending a convention in Indianapolis about mass evangelism. Inspired by the stirring messages he was hearing about winning the lost, he went with his song leader to the street corner during an intermission that evening. The song leader stood on a box and began to sing. When a crowd had gathered, the evangelist began to preach. Soon so many people had assembled that the throng was spilling into the streets. The evangelist thought it best to invite the people to follow him to the nearby convention hall where the evangelism conference was being held. Soon the auditorium was filled with spiritually hungry people, and the evangelist began to preach the gospel to them passionately.

After a while the convention delegates returned from their dinner break to find street people now occupying some of their reserved seats. The delegates began to mutter and complain amongst themselves. The nerve of this evangelist to impose himself this way—who does he think he is? The convention leaders deliberated about what should be done and then sent a representative to the evangelist to tell him their verdict. The evangelist was in mid-sermon when the messenger approached and whispered into his ear. The evangelist stopped preaching and said to the crowd who had come to hear the gospel, "Now we must close, as the brethren of the convention wish to come and discuss the topic 'How to Reach the Masses.'"

There always seems to be a great divide in life between action and intention, between works and words, between doing something and merely talking about doing it. And it is in this space, between desire and deed, where most people die in a wilderness of inaction. For every go-getter who is ready to take the field, there are a thousand professional conference delegates who are content to go on endlessly discussing the need without ever actually doing anything. But the ones who will go on to see God's will fulfilled in their lives are people of action, initiative, and urgency.

In the Christian world many people spend their whole lives waiting for God to do something for them. They talk about waiting for God's timing or provision; they are looking for God to "make a way," "open doors," and give "divine appointments." Although there will certainly be situations in life when we need to wait for the Lord, many times (perhaps even most times, if we are honest) the real underlying reason for our inaction is far less spiritual than we would like to believe. In the secular world people have the same hang-ups, except instead of "waiting for God" they are waiting for "the right moment" or "the perfect opportunity." For saint and sinner alike these perfect moments almost never come.

A young woman told her pastor she wanted to attend a certain Bible college. With whimsical indifference she told him she wasn't sure when she would go. She said there were quite a number of obstacles in her way (mostly financial), and she believed that if it was really God's will, He would "prepare the way" for her. In other words, she thought that if she was really supposed to attend this Bible college, God would solve all of her problems, pay all of her bills, and roll out a red carpet for her. This kind of thinking should make you want to stand on a table and scream!

Where is the urgency? Where is the passion? Where is the chutzpah? If you want God to part the sea for you but you are not even willing to get your toes wet, you are living in a fantasy world—this is simply not the way it works. Even when God is fully in something and has ordained it, He rarely arranges all the aspects of our lives so that everything is perfect and easy. On the contrary, in many cases God's will for your life will seem like the more difficult path, and it will have to be pursued with real determination. Jesus said, "The kingdom of heaven suffereth violence, and the violent take it by force" (Matt. 11:12, KJV). God is looking for the burning-hearted, not the faint-hearted.

Daniel 11:32 tell us, "But the people who know their God shall stand firm and take action" (ESV). Anyone who knows God and understands His ways will know that God expects us to take action. God cannot bless our good intentions, only what we actually do!

Jesus told a parable in Matthew 21:28–31. "There was a man who had two sons. He went to the first and said, 'Son, go and work today in the vineyard.' 'I will not,' he answered, but later he changed his mind and went. Then the father went to the other son and said the same thing. He answered, 'I will, sir,' but he did not go. Which of the two did what his father wanted? 'The first,' they answered" (NIV).

The moral of the story is clear: good intentions and empty promises are not enough. God is looking for men and women of action! "Be doers of the word," James says, "and not hearers only" (James 1:22).

Second Corinthians 9:10 says God gives seed to the sower. God's way is counter-intuitive. We would say, "God should first provide the seed, then I will sow."

But God says, "Sow first, and then I will provide the seed." While we are waiting for God to provide, God is waiting for us to act. It is our demonstrated faith that moves God's heart and hand, not just our need.

## GET MOVING

In order to fly, an airplane needs "lift." Lift comes from speed, and speed comes from "thrust." Thrust is the power that pushes the air craft forward, and without it nothing else matters. The aerodynamic design, the well-trained pilot in the cockpit, the sophisticated navigational technology, and the tank full of jet fuel are all useless unless the engines come alive and provide forward motion. In your life the only one who can provide the forward motion is you. God will be your pilot. He will provide the wind beneath your wings and the fuel in your tank, but you have to give Him some momentum to work with. You cannot do God's part, and God will not do your part. Your part is to get into gear, get off your backside, and get moving. Evangelist Reinhard Bonnke has said, "God will lift you out of the deepest pit, but He won't lift you out of an easy chair—you have to do that yourself." So what are you waiting for? How long will you do nothing while you grow old in the wilderness of inaction?

It is true that God opens doors, and sometimes particular doors are not opened for a variety of reasons. But it is very unlikely that all the doors are shut. Imagine a man sitting at a red light in the downtown area of a big city. The light in front of him turns green, but when he looks ahead he sees that the next five lights are still red. Should he sit at the green light in front of him and just wait for all the other lights to turn green as well? Of course not! He should move through the green light he has. Yet many people fail to move through the green light God has given them because they foresee obstacles ahead that they don't know how to handle.

In Joshua 3 we read about the children of Israel encountering the obstacle of the Jordan River, which was overflowing and impossible to cross. In obedience to the Lord, Joshua told the priests to take the ark of the covenant and go forward into the waters of the Jordan.

This surely would have seemed like a ridiculous idea, but look at what happened.

> And when those who carried the ark came into the Jordan, and the feet of the priests carrying the ark were dipped in the edge of the water...the waters which were flowing down

> from above stood and rose up in one heap....So
> the people crossed opposite Jericho.
>
> —JOSHUA 3:15–16, NAS

Now if Joshua had been trained in one of our fine Bible colleges, he probably would have given more mature advice. He would have said, "Gentlemen, we are going to wait right here until the Lord 'opens a door' for us." But if that had been his command, their skeletons would still be decomposing somewhere on the banks of the Jordan River, because the water was not going to part for them until their feet got wet! My friend, sometimes you need to just go ahead and get your feet wet in faith and see what the Lord will do for you!

In Matthew 14:22–29 we read the story of how Peter walked on the water. It was early in the morning when Jesus came walking toward the disciples' boat on the turbulent sea. When the disciples saw Him, they thought it was a ghost and they cried out in fear, but Jesus said, "Be of good cheer. It is I. Do not be afraid."

"Lord, if it is You," Peter replied, "bid me come to You on the water."

"Come," He said.

Notice that Jesus didn't say, "Peter, come." He simply said, "Come." Do you realize what this means? Any of the disciples could have responded to that word and walked on the water. People often criticize Peter for taking his eyes off Jesus and sinking, but I admire him for being the only one willing to get out of the boat. You will never walk on water if you're not willing to step out of the boat!

This secret is so simple and yet underemphasized in the Christian world. Some people seem to think that taking action demonstrates a lack of faith. On the contrary, faith without works is dead! Said another way, faith without action is dead! All of the planning, waiting, and wishing is wasted time if you are not going to take action. If you want to learn to swim, you are going to have to go ahead and take the plunge.

We are usually all too aware of our inadequacies and deficiencies. The best way to address these issues is to begin to move forward. Momentum and motion will make everything in your life easier to steer. As you move forward, you'll discover what really needs your attention, you'll be incentivized to deal with it urgently, you'll make the needed adjustments, and you'll be able to empirically gauge your progress. You'll discover that many of your previous concerns were nonsense and that you had never even considered many of the real issues you needed to confront.

Jack Canfield, the very successful businessman and

author, wrote about this secret in his best-selling book *The Success Principles*: "Successful people have a bias for action. Most successful people I know have a low tolerance for excessive planning and talking about it. They are antsy to get going. They want to get started. They want the games to begin....Planning has its place, but it must be kept in perspective. Some people spend their whole lives waiting for the perfect time to do something. There's rarely a 'perfect' time to do anything. What is important is to just get started. Get into the game. Get on the playing field. Once you do, you will start to get feedback that will help you make the corrections you need to make to be successful."[1]

## READY, FIRE, AIM

A man and his father went to the shooting range. The father was heading out on a hunting trip, and before he left his son wanted to help him "sight in" the rifle he had bought him as a gift. The pair looked through the scope, which they had just attached, aimed at the target, and fired, knowing they would most likely miss the bull's-eye. But by firing at the target, they could see how they needed to adjust to the scope. They were only able to make corrections when they saw how they were missing the mark.

This is typical of life. We usually learn more from our mistakes than our successes. But unless you fire, you will never miss, and unless you miss, you will never be able to make the adjustments necessary to hit the bull's-eye.

Whenever a certain businessman begins a new project or initiative, he never views his initial plan as the final draft. He dives into it knowing that he will learn as he goes. This means that he's not paralyzed by a fear of failure; rather he looks forward to learning what not to do. He sees the initial plan is an uncalibrated machine with many dials. The dials are all the different variables represented in that particular project. Once the machine is running, he can see what is working and what is not working. After gathering sufficient feedback, he will tweak the "dials" based on that feedback.

Even when everything seems to be running smoothly, this man will step back often to analyze the process. If something is working well, he will try to capitalize on it. If something is not working well, he will adjust it or prune it off altogether. It is an ongoing dynamic development that never ends. This process is where real progress is made, but until you take action, all of your planning and strategizing is simply untested theory.

With all these things in mind, remember this: taking action is not just a matter of trial and error. At its core, it is a matter of faithfulness. Even if there are a thousand things you cannot do for one reason or another, there is always something you can do. It may seem small or insignificant, but the eyes of God are on you. He is watching to see what you will do with the opportunities He has given you, and your response will determine whether He entrusts you with more.

An evangelist preached a sermon in a church once and afterward a young man came up to him with tears in his eyes and said, "I have a calling like yours. The Lord has called me to preach the gospel. I believe I am going to win millions of people to the Lord, but I don't know where to start." The evangelist put an arm around the young man and said, "I think I can help you." He said, "You can?" The evangelist said, "Yes, I can tell you where to start. Start by telling your unsaved family members about Jesus. Then go and tell your unsaved friends about Jesus. Then go out to the street corners and preach the gospel to lost people wherever you can find them. As God sees your faithfulness, He will give you more."

Another young man shared his vision with his mentor one day. He said, "I am going to start a house of prayer. I am going to have prayer, intercession, and worship going on twenty-four hours per day, seven days per week, three hundred sixty-five days per year."

"That's a wonderful vision," his mentor said. "When will it begin?" He said, "Well, first I need to gather several dozen worship bands together and several hundred intercessors who share my vision."

The mentor could see a problem in his plan right away. "Can I give you some advice?" he asked. The young man was very eager to hear it. The mentor said, "Why don't you start with one evening per week or one day per month? Start by doing whatever you can do, and as you are faithful, God will give you more."

Unfortunately the mentor's advice was too unexciting for the young man. He decided to wait until all the bands and intercessors had been assembled. Sadly, several years later, he still had not started the house of prayer.

Few people start out in ministry by preaching to millions of people. They begin by preaching to a few wherever they are.

There's an ancient Chinese proverb that says, "The journey of a thousand miles begins with the first step." Perhaps you don't know how to get from A to Z, but you don't need to know that. All you need to know is how to get from A to B. Once you get to B, then you will go to C, and one step at a time you will find that the waters will begin to part as your feet get wet.

## CHAPTER 8

# CONSIDER WHAT IS ALREADY IN YOUR HAND

I T IS INTERESTING that when people ultimately discover what God has called them to do, often they look back and see that God had placed many things in their lives early on to prepare them for their calling. It might have been a natural talent or ability. It might have been certain interests. It may have been people who influenced them in the direction of their calling, even if they didn't recognize it at the time. It may have been an event or an experience that propelled them toward the plans God had for them. One thing is certain: God always prepares us for the things He has in store for us.

When God called Moses to deliver the children of Israel out of Egypt, Moses was thoroughly overwhelmed. His mind was filled with questions, and he could not even imagine how he would begin to accomplish such a feat. He began to bombard God with questions, concerns, and objections, but God did not say, "Don't worry, Moses. This is what I'm going to do. First, I'm going to turn the waters of the Nile into blood. Then I'll send a plague of frogs followed by a plague of lice followed by a plague of flies. Then I'll kill the livestock, send boils, hail and locusts, then follow that up with darkness and death of the first-born. Once you're out of Egypt, I'll part the Red Sea and lead you through the wilderness with a pillar of cloud by day and a pillar of fire by night."

A detailed revelation of God's plan probably would have been a great comfort to Moses. Instead when Moses asked all his frantic questions about how God would deliver His people, God responded with a question of His own. "Moses, what is in your hand?" And Moses replied, "A rod."

Think for a minute about the absurdity of what God was asking Moses to do. He was sending this fugitive vagabond into the most powerful empire in the world to deliver His people. And all Moses had as ammunition was a stick! Through the whole Exodus saga—all the miracles, wonders, and epic, world-changing exploits—Moses had nothing more in his hand than a stick! But when Moses did what he knew to do, when he used what was in his hand, the rest of the story began to unfold, each event triggering the next like a succession of dominoes leading all the way to the Promised Land.

Take an inventory of your life today to see what is in your hand right now. It may be people, relationships, interests, opportunities, thoughts, or dreams. Chances are that the seeds of your future have already been sown into the soil of your life.

## DISCOVER YOUR STRENGTHS

God has given all of us gifts, and often He put those strengths within us because He wants us to use them to fulfill His purpose for our lives. So part of seeking God about His will for your life is knowing what our gifts, talents, and strengths are.

For years we were told to strengthen our weaknesses, but more and more social scientists are finding that our weaker areas will become only so strong no matter how much we work on them. Yet when we build up our strengths, they become even stronger, and often we are able to excel in that area far beyond our expectations.

You have the ability to rapidly become even better at the things you're already good at, so take some time to explore what those strengths are. Here are two resources that can help you get started:

- The Gallup Strength Center (www
  .gallupstrengthscenter.com) offers an
  inexpensive self-assessment that will
  help you identify your five greatest
  strengths along with action points that
  will help you further strengthen those
  areas.

- The DiSC Personality Profile (www
  .thediscpersonalitytest.com) helps you
  learn how you are wired. Though it
  focuses on your personality, not your
  strengths, if you can understand how
  you're wired, you will be able to better
  identify your strengths. Understanding
  your personality will help you develop
  your gifts and find the activities that suit
  you best.

## SOW WHAT YOU WANT TO REAP

Even when you know what God's will is for your life,
you may have to wait for it to be fulfilled. As you wait,
remember that you are planting seeds right now that
will determine what you will reap tomorrow. Your
attitude is a seed. Your time is a seed. Your prayers
are seeds. One common reason people get frustrated

is that they begin planting good seeds, yet they are not seeing the fruit they want.

Some time ago a man decided it was time to get back in shape. He bought a set of exercise videos that had come highly recommended. The very first day of his new regimen, his wife and six-year-old decided to join him in exercising. About five minutes into the video—still somewhere in the stretches—the man's son turned to him with great excitement and said, "Hey, Dad, look. You almost got muscles. Look at your elbows!"

The man and his wife had a real good laugh, but the poor little boy never understood what was so funny. No one had the heart to tell him it doesn't work that way. It takes a long time and many doughnuts to get out of shape. And getting fit, losing weight, and building muscle doesn't happen overnight either—much less after a few minutes of warming up. The little boy didn't quite understand the principle of sowing and reaping, and unfortunately many adults don't either.

After service one Sunday a church member approached the pastor obviously disgruntled. "Pastor," the man said, "the Bible says to 'test God' with the tithe and offering, and that's exactly what I did." He went on to explain that before he became a Christian and started attending the church, his family had been going through a season of great financial hardship.

Now that he was learning about the Bible, he read Malachi's guarantee that the "windows of heaven" would be opened over those who give.

The past Sunday he decided to "test God." He emptied out his wallet in the offering plate and gave for the first time. But the subsequent week was not as he had anticipated. His financial difficulties continued, and he was concerned that there was something wrong with the Bible. He had sown a seed but had not reaped a harvest.

This man's mistake was a basic misunderstanding of how sowing and reaping works, much like the little boy when he was examining his father's elbows for muscle sprouts five minutes into their first workout. The pastor explained to this gentleman that whatever you are harvesting now is not the result of what you planted a few hours ago.

Today you are reaping what you planted months ago, even years ago, in a different season. Likewise the seeds you plant today won't necessarily be ready for harvest by the next day or even by next Sunday.

Imagine what it may have been like to grow up on an ancient Israeli farm. The long winter months have reduced the once plentiful pantries to empty shelves, and the family is now living on meager rations and dreaming about a loaf of bread fresh from the oven.

Suddenly the rain begins to pour, and the once-dusty fields are becoming rivers. The father says to his young son, "Come, it's time to sow." Together they walk out to the barn where the father climbs into the loft and pulls down huge bags of grain.

"Father!" the young boy exclaims, "now we can make bread!" The father replies, "No, my son. This grain is not for eating. Come, I will show you what it is for." He fills a sack with grain, and they wade into the flooded fields. Then the father does the most absurd thing; he begins throwing the grain into the water! That night at the dinner table, the little boy eats his paltry portion and wonders why his father threw all that grain away. Many weeks will go by before he understands, but one day the water will recede and the little boy will step outside and behold a miracle. The fields will be full of tiny sprouts, racing heavenward to produce a harvest of golden grain. It was this ancient farming technique that Solomon was referring to when he wrote, "Cast your bread upon the waters, for you will find it after many days" (Eccles. 11:1).

Throwing perfectly good grain into the water when you are hungry is a difficult thing to do, but what is more difficult is waiting many days for the harvest. This is why Paul encourages us by saying, "Let us not grow weary in doing good, for *in due season* we shall reap, if we do not give up" (Gal. 6:9, emphasis added).

It is amazing and sobering to think that we are all planting seeds all the time. Sowing and reaping are not confined to putting money in an offering plate. That cheeseburger you ate, that movie you watched, that comment you made, that time you spent with your family, that book you read—everything you do is a seed that will produce a harvest (good or bad) in the future. Be careful what you plant in this season because you will eat it in the next.

In the end our lives are a sum total of the decisions we have made—a harvest, if you will, of what we have sown. You can't usually change today's harvest by sowing good seeds today, but if you will determine to sow the right seeds day in and day out, in "due season" you will reap your harvest if you "faint not."

Even if you find yourself waiting for the fulfillment of God's promise for your life, keep sowing good seeds and beware of impatience. Allow God to do the work in your heart that He is trying to accomplish. The children of Israel walked in circles in the wilderness decade after decade because they did not learn their lesson. Some people keep going in circles because they never learn what God is trying to teach them, and they never move to the next phase because they never pass the test. Stop squirming and wiggling and trying to get through with this as quickly as possible, but be faithful and patient. When you pass the test, He will lead you forward.

Another way to put the law of sowing and reaping to work for you is to find someone else who has a vision from the Lord and invest into that person's vision as if it were your own. Volunteer your time, energy, and resources to push someone else forward. You will find that as you sow into someone else's vision, you will soon reap a vision of your own.

## Be Faithful Where You Find Yourself

It used to be standard practice for large companies to "headhunt" talented executives from prestigious universities or other successful companies for senior positions. But more and more I have noticed that it is becoming the policy of many large companies to promote from within. They look for talented people from their own ranks, individuals who have proven their trustworthiness and worked their way up the ladder, even from very low positions. This has always been God's preferred method of promotion. God looks for faithful people He can promote and bless. He tests us with small tasks to see how we will react, and when we have proven ourselves, He gives us bigger responsibilities.

Moses had one of the most important leadership positions in history. He was assigned the challenging task of leading an entire nation—God's chosen people, no less—across the wilderness to the Promised Land. It's interesting to think that before God appointed Moses to such an important role, Moses had a similar assignment but on a much smaller scale. Rather than leading people through the wilderness, he was leading a flock of stinky sheep through that very same wilderness—for forty years! How could God have trusted Moses to lead His people if Moses had not proven His faithfulness leading sheep?

We see this principle articulated over and over in Jesus's teaching. In the parable of the talents Jesus says to the servant who had doubled his investment, "Well done, you good and faithful servant. You have been faithful over a few things. I will make you ruler over many things" (Matt. 25:21). In another parable Jesus said, "He who is faithful in what is least is faithful also in much. And he who is dishonest in the least is dishonest also in much" (Luke 16:10). He goes on to compare the servant's ability to handle money with his ability to handle "true riches": "So if you have not been faithful in the unrighteous wealth, who will commit to your trust the true riches? And if you have not been faithful in that which is another man's, who will give you that which is your own?" (Luke 16:11–12).

Psalm 75:6–7 says, "For neither from the east nor west, nor from the wilderness comes victory. But God is the judge; He brings one low, and lifts up another." The scripture is clear: promotion does not come from the horizontal plane—the east or the west. That is to say that men are not the source of promotion. Also, promotion does not come from the south; the devil is also not the source of promotion. If promotion comes not from the south, east, or west, we know by process of elimination from which direction promotion comes—north! Look up! God is the promoter, and He promotes those who are faithful.

# CHAPTER 9

# DON'T LOSE FOCUS

IN 2 SAMUEL 23 we read about David's "mighty men," a small militia of extraordinarily skilled warriors. It was not a big army, but it was a tough army, like a highly trained Special Forces unit. They were amazingly proficient with their weapons. In fact, the Bible says they could split a hair with their slingshots—left-handed! (See 1 Chronicles 12:2.) The chapter goes on to describe in greater detail the exploits of a small handful within that group who were the best of the best of the best!

These men were like real-life superheroes who would make Rambo look like a Girl Scout. One of these men was Adino, "on account of eight hundred slain on one occasion" (2 Sam. 23:8). "Abishai...wielded his spear against three hundred men and killed them" (v. 18). Benaiah the son of Jehoiada "went down and killed a lion in the middle of a pit on a snowy day. He struck down an Egyptian, an impressive man. Now the Egyptian had a spear in his hand, but Benaiah went down to him with a staff, seized the spear from the Egyptian, and killed him with his own spear" (vv. 20–21).

But one of the most interesting for the purpose of our discussion is Shammah.

> Now after him was Shammah the son of Agee a Hararite. And the Philistines were gathered into a troop where there was a plot of ground full of lentils, and the people fled from the Philistines. But he took his stand in the midst of the plot, defended it and struck the Philistines; and the LORD brought about a great victory.
>
> —2 SAMUEL 23:11–12, NAS

Some scholars believe Shammah could be the same man whom Judges 3:31 calls Shamgar, who killed six hundred Philistines with an ox goad! Either way one thing is clear: Shammah won an overwhelming victory against impossible odds, and through his courage and valor, God brought about a great triumph for Israel.

It is interesting that 2 Samuel 23:12 tells us exactly where Shammah strategically positioned himself. It says, "He stationed himself in the middle of the field" (NKJV). He wasn't standing out on the fringes, and he wasn't in one of the corners. He was right in the very center of the field. I have seen many people who were called to a particular field, but over the years they became distracted. They lost their focus and wandered to the fringes of their field and sometimes even drifted into other fields they were never called to serve. If you are going to remain in the center of God's will for your life, you must resolve to stand in the middle of the field to which He has called you and remain focused without allowing the enemy to distract you from that call.

Through the Holy Spirit we are equipped to live fruitful and effective lives, accomplishing all that God has for us to do. The devil is no match for the Spirit of God who lives within us. Greater is He who is in us than he that is in the world. But the enemy has a secret weapon—distraction. If the devil can't stop us, he will attempt to derail us with one distraction and then another. The devil knows something we so often forget—that we are in a race against time. Every minute we are distracted from what God has called us to do is a minute closer to the end of the fight. The devil will even use "good" things as distractions if he can to keep us from the best things that God has in store.

In James 4:14 our lives are described as "a vapor that appears for a little while and then vanishes away." There are not enough hours in a day to do everything. There are not enough years in your life to live for everything. There is not enough blood in your veins to bleed for everything. That's why it is so important that you choose your battles wisely, don't get distracted and sacrifice what is "best" on the altar of what is "good."

In 1 Corinthians 9:24 Paul encourages us to run the race of our lives "in such a way that you may win" (NAS). A person who is running to win sets his eyes on the finish line and goes for it with all his might. A person who is running to win has made a choice to lay down everything else for the sake of the prize.

Evangelist Reinhard Bonnke once told the story of how a newspaper had spread vicious lies about him. His friends, jealous for his reputation, urged him to respond. But when he prayed, the Lord spoke to him and said, "You are My harvest worker. Don't stop the combine harvester just to catch a mouse!"

There are a lot of good battles out there to fight, and the devil would be happy if you would get involved in every one of them, because if he can keep you distracted chasing mice, he can rob you of your harvest. John Maxwell wrote, "At age sixty I now look back at my youth and I cringe at my naïveté. My toolbox of experience had only one tool in it: a hammer. If all you have is a hammer, everything looks like a nail. So I pounded and pounded. I fought many battles I shouldn't have."[1]

Years ago a friend of mine became fascinated with a particular doctrinal debate. Although it was an issue of little or no real-life consequence, he was so sure he was right that he started an ongoing argument within the church where he was on staff. The pastor, realizing that this debate was causing more harm than good, asked him to drop it. He refused, choosing rather to forfeit his job and ministry. This story would not be worth sharing if it were the only time I have seen this. But I could point to several people who are out of ministry today because they were derailed by something petty. Somehow they lost sight of the big harvest and started chasing mice.

Paul exhorts us to "avoid foolish controversies and genealogies and arguments and quarrels about the law, because these are unprofitable and useless" (Titus 3:9, NIV). Notice that Paul did not call these controversies, arguments, and quarrels sinful things; he called them unprofitable and useless things. Even if something is not necessarily a sin, it can still distract us from what is important. That is why Paul was exhorting us not to get distracted but to stay focused on what is useful and profitable.

I've seen pastors who spent more time doing construction projects at their churches than they spent pastoring their people. I have seen ministries of evangelists whom God called to preach the gospel of salvation transform into humanitarian organizations. I have seen people who have been gifted in particular areas decide to follow more lucrative paths that took them away from their calling. These are all examples of the ways the enemy can distract us from God's will for our lives. It's not that the distractions are necessarily bad things. In fact, sometimes they are wonderful things. But if they keep us from the best thing—doing God's will—the enemy has succeeded.

We've been talking a lot about God's will for your life, but remember, the devil also has a plan for you, and his plan is to make you ineffective and unfruitful. He would love for you to park your combine harvester to chase mice. If he cannot block you, he will try to derail you. He will try to distract you from your assignment. Ignore him. Keep your eyes on the prize, keep fighting in the middle of your field, and run your race in such a way that you will win!

## STAND FIRM AND DON'T LET GO

We all want to discover God's will for our lives, but once we discover it, that is not the end; it is only the beginning! Once you have your assignment from God, then you have to stand in your field as Shammah did and fight until God gives the victory. This requires a quality that few seem to possess—perseverance.

In Ephesians 6 we are commanded to "put on the

whole armor of God" (v. 11). But verses 13 and 14 say something important: "And having done all, to stand. Stand therefore." In other words, after you have made all the preparation to stand, now there is one thing left to do—stand! This is where many people miss it. They go to great lengths to discover God's will for their lives. They go to Bible college; they read books; they receive prophetic words; they prepare themselves in every way possible. But when their skin begins to burn with the heat of the battle, they drop their weapons and retreat.

We are always looking for shortcuts, tips, and tricks, but there is no way around this principle. You can be extraordinarily gifted, talented, anointed, and blessed, but without persistence you will have little impact because the great victories are always on the other side of great battles. The word *persevere* is made of the prefix *per*, which means "through," and *severe*. Victory comes to those who press through severe battles to the other side without quitting.

R. Alec Mackenzie, who wrote extensively on the subject of time management, said, "The ability to concentrate—to persevere on a course without distraction or diversion—is a power that has enabled men of moderate capability to reach heights of attainment that have eluded the genius. They have no secret formula other than to persevere."[2]

Helen Hayes won many prestigious awards during her acting career, which spanned nearly seventy years. But she attributed her success not to talent or ability: "Nothing is any good without endurance."[3] Chemist Louis Pasteur, who developed the disease-preventing process that came to be called pasteurization, said, "My strength lies solely in my tenacity."[4]

When it comes to fulfilling God's will for your life, perseverance is not an option; it is an imperative. If you let go of God's calling, you will never fulfill it.

What do you do when the going gets tough? Stand firm and don't let go! What do you do when the enemy begins to assail from all directions? Stand firm and don't let go! What do you do when you face financial difficulty, health problems, betrayal, abandonment, rejection, and pain? Stand firm and don't let go! My friend, the battle belongs to the Lord, and He will win it in His time. Our part is not to question; our part is to obey and stand firm until God gives the victory.

Never give up! Never retreat! Never surrender to the enemy! Your fulfillment of God's will for your life is not only about you. It's also about your children and your grandchildren and the future of God's eternal kingdom. So stand! Fight! And endure until the end. And God will give you the victory in Jesus's name!

## CHAPTER 10

# REMEMBER THE WHY
# BEHIND THE WHAT

ONCE A FAMOUS movie star was being interviewed. The host asked him how it felt to finally make it in the movies after dreaming about it from the time he was a child and overcoming so many trials to achieve his goals. The actor surprised everyone with his answer: "It's boring." He said, "My whole life I dreamt of doing films, and now I find it's boring."

He was shocked that the thing that had driven him and shaped him left him empty when he attained it. The stories go on and on of people who have been motivated by a temporary dream, only to attain it and then feel empty and aimless. Many others never attain their earthly dream, and they live in great pain over it. Their entire lives they dream of becoming something, and when they cannot get it, they feel like failures.

Our primary purpose in life must exceed temporary attainments, goals, and dreams. Our true purpose in life is connected to a dream that is unbreakable and inexhaustible, yet attainable. It is a dream that moves forward and is so vast that it has no end. It is a life dream that will sustain you both now and forever.

This dream is found in the eyes of the "Audience of One." Ultimately we must find our purpose in the eyes of Jesus. People love you one minute and ridicule you the next. One year you're cool, and the next you're outdated. One season you are successful, and the next you are a failure. This is true in finances, relationships, ministry, impact, influence; everything in life is on a quick fade.

We cannot anchor our purpose to these things, because it would be like chasing the wind. Though these things are important and relevant, they are secondary and not the anchor of our lives. When we live before His eyes and seek to be pleasing to Him, above all else, then everything we do in life has purpose and eternal significance.

The most important thing is what Jesus thinks of us. That is what matters.

## Aim to Please Him

In 2 Corinthians 5:9 the Apostle Paul said, "We make it our aim...to be well pleasing to Him" (NKJV). We want Him pleased because He is the Creator. We were created for His pleasure, and we will never be satisfied until we satisfy Him.

There was a moment in Paul's life when he consciously determined that the primary dream of his life would be to be pleasing to God. He determined this would be the supreme preoccupation of his life, walking with the Lord and living his entire life to be well pleasing to Him. To "make it his aim" means it is the primary reason he had life on the earth. He is not saying, "I made this one of my top ten things on my to-do list." No, this was the primary ambition of his life.

We have many dreams in our hearts that are biblical and of God. We have dreams related to ministry, money, marriage, health, and impacting others. We have dreams and promises related to these very important subjects. They are biblical, and they are important to God, but they must be of secondary importance to this one, primary aim.

Nobody can make this your aim. It must be your choice. This is why it is powerful to the heart of God, because it is voluntary. There are many people who know Jesus as Savior and will be in heaven, but they lived their lives without giving much further thought to Him. They are saved and please Him in the sense that they have the free gift of righteousness, but there is another element of pleasing Him that comes when we set our hearts to live wholeheartedly before Him. This is what Paul was talking about. Once you determine this is your primary life dream, you have to make it your aim and align yourself to walk in harmony with this goal.

It is natural for us as human beings to get disoriented and distracted from this aim. Over and over we must stop and realign our hearts to make this the primary ambition of our lives. When you picture your future, don't just picture yourself in love with a happy family, lots of money, and lots of friends—the typical American dream. These are good things, but there is more to your life than this. When you think of twenty or thirty years from now, do you have a dream to be walking in a way, in both heart and action, that is pleasing in God's sight? This is the primary picture you should have of your life when you think about your future. Yes, money, relationships, family, and ministry are valid desires in the will of God, but there is a bigger definition of success that is beyond these things.

## WE ARE WELL KNOWN TO GOD

Paul wrote in 2 Corinthians 5:11 that "we are well known to God" (NKJV). He not only understood he had a great purpose; he also understood that the judge, the one evaluating him, was deeply invested in the details of his life. If we know Jesus is engaged and cares about the efforts we are making that nobody else cares about...if we know He sees the small acts of obedience...if we believe we are well known to Him, that He really cares about these things and remembers them, writes them in His books and rewards us forever, then our lives change. If we know we have an appointment to stand before our Creator and the Creator Himself knows even the intricacies of our lives and what we do matters to Him, then we have purpose.

King David said God fashioned our hearts individually and He considers our works (Ps. 33:15). This means He sees what we are doing and actually thinks about it and ponders it. David also wrote of how God searched him and knew him (Ps. 139:1). This was the power driving David's life. Like Paul, he knew God knew him well and was paying attention. This is a stunning reality to those who believe it.

Our responsiveness to God is what we are measured

by. He does not measure how big your ministry is or how big your bank account is or how high your IQ is. He doesn't even measure how many people you are able to impact. He measures the size of your heart. This is the true measure of a man.

Someone could be far more gifted and impact many more people than you, but if your responsiveness is the same, you get the same reward. To be rewarded means there is an appointed day in history when Jesus wants to communicate openly to you, and to others, how He feels about the way you loved Him. What a tragedy it would be on that day for Him to have little to say about the way you lived on the earth.

When we have the confidence that He is attentive and remembers even the smallest words spoken and rewards the smallest reach toward Him, when we believe Jesus is this attentive and this eager, we will want to please Him. Our purpose is found in His eyes. The burning desire to please God must be the primary ambition of our lives.

The Apostle Paul's dream was unbreakable. He could be in prison, he could be in front of a multitude, or he could be suffering great persecution. Still Paul had a deep desire to be pleasing in Jesus's sight, and he kept his eyes on this prize knowing that wisdom would be justified (Matt. 11:19). It was his primary goal, and he often spoke of it and wrote about it. This was the dream that kept him steady through persecution and promotion. He counted it all as loss—the good and the bad. This desire to be pleasing in Jesus's sight creates humility and steadfastness in a person.

> Not that I have already attained or have already been perfected, but I follow after it so that I may lay hold of that for which I was seized by Christ Jesus. Brothers, I do not count myself to have attained, but this one thing I do, forgetting those things which are behind and reaching forward to those things which are ahead, I press toward the goal to the prize of the high calling of God in Christ Jesus.
>
> —PHILIPPIANS 3:12–14

## ETERNALLY GREAT

A person who lives determined to be well pleasing to God is able to become eternally great no matter what this life has given him (Matt. 5:19). This is true liberation. No one can touch a man or a woman who lives like this. Their money can be taken, they can lose relationships and positions, and they can be thrown into prison, persecuted, or even martyred. Still they will attain what they are aiming for. A person can be uneducated and unattractive, sitting on the back row where nobody notices him. This person has the same capacity to be as eternally great in God's eyes as the person who is the most educated, beautiful, and seemingly successful in the eyes of man today.

God does not measure us as people measure us. Paul knew this. Church history is full of men and women who were free because they lived to please Jesus even when they were thrown into prison for their faith. History proves that the power and worth of a person comes from whether we choose to live to be pleasing to God, and anyone and everyone can do it. Anybody, everybody, who wants to be eternally great can be, and we are not at the mercy of the rise and fall of external favor and blessing.

Our definition of greatness is not affected by our assignment in life. We have assignments that are important, and we serve in these assignments with faithfulness, but these do not determine our success. We cannot build our confidence on them. Our confidence is in serving in our assignment before the Audience of One.

The issue is whose applause we are living for. People do not burn out because their assignment is too difficult. They burn out because they are doing their assignment before the wrong set of eyes, looking for the wrong applause. The heart is often revealed when we are criticized. If we are thrown off by criticism, we are living before the wrong eyes.

Failure is another test. When our life assignments seem to fail—we lose money, our ministries shrink, or our relationships fail—of course we feel the pain. But if we are devastated by these things, concluding that our whole life is a failure because of them, it is proof we are not living before the Audience of One. We are living for the applause of man. Many times Jesus will test our hearts in this way to show us where our true value lies. We must realign ourselves again and again to live for His pleasure.

## OUR PRIMARY PURPOSE

This primary purpose of our lives to please Jesus must become our compulsion and our consuming dream. We want to be preoccupied with Jesus and less occupied with the opinion of man. This is the prize that is set before us, and it must be the anchor of our souls. Nothing can take this dream away from you when it is your primary motivation, and it can be attained no matter what life circumstance you are in.

It doesn't matter what sphere you have been given. You could be on the backside of nowhere and have only two or three people who are listening to you, or you could be on a stage in front of millions. You could be healthy, full of charisma and charm, so that people naturally follow you, or you could be ill and unable to communicate clearly. You can be rich or poor, beautiful or not. You can be educated or uneducated, from any nationality, any social background and still fulfill the vision Jesus has for you and therefore be eternally great and successful at fulfilling your life purpose.

A person's true measure is found in Jesus's eyes. You may never be great in the eyes of man, but there is one man who sees, and He is so attentive to you that He knows your thoughts and your deepest emotions (1 Cor. 4:5). He sees all and judges all, and His evaluation is what matters. His evaluation of you is what will define you for billions of years.

This makes life today powerful. Not only is there a man who is fully God who is attentive to you, but He also promises to reward you. Every act of love you give Him will be rewarded in the age to come, and only then will the truth about you be seen.

Right now you are in the "womb of eternity," and you are being fashioned for a day that is yet to come. The pressure, the pain, the pleasure, and the blessings are all part of the Creator's plan to form and fashion you into the image of His love. But it must be love defined by Jesus, not by humanism. He is looking for love on His terms. What is that definition? What pleases Him?

When asked what was the greatest commandment, Jesus said, "'You shall love the Lord your God with all your heart, and with all your soul, and with all your mind.' This is the first and great commandment. And the second is like it: 'You shall love your neighbor as yourself'" (Matt. 22:36–39).

This commandment reflects God's ultimate purpose for Creation. Jesus the great teacher, the great prophet, the great philosopher, the great psychologist, and God Himself is saying that loving Him is first in priority to Him and to His Father. It is the preeminent command and the pinnacle of all that He has spoken. When we love Him with this kind of wholeness, we are what we were created to be. We fulfill our primary purpose in this love. It is the great commandment, and it is the greatest calling.

Some who seek to know God's will for their life focus on knowing what they are supposed to do instead of who they are supposed to become. When they speak of wanting the greatest calling, they refer to the size of their ministry instead of the size of their heart. The greatest grace we can receive is the anointing to feel

God's love and to express it. This brings the greatest freedom and has the greatest reward.

Our purpose in life is to please Jesus, and in Matthew 22 He tells us what pleases Him: it is when we love Him with all our heart, soul, mind, and strength, and pour this love out to others. Jesus made the way to please Him so simple that anyone can do it, yet many don't. God's purpose for our lives is not too mysterious or far away. It is to live for His pleasure and remain steadfast in this pursuit.

# NOTES

## CHAPTER 1
### BELIEVE GOD HAS A PLAN FOR YOUR LIFE

1. Greg Ogden, *Discipleship Essentials* (Downers Grove, IL: InterVarsity Press, 1998).

2. Healthsolution.in, "You Use 200 Muscles to Take One Step," accessed March 21, 2012, http://tinyurl.com/7s5y89g.

3. Emmett L. Williams and George Mulfinger Jr., *Physical Science for Christian Schools* (Greenville, SC: Bob Jones University Press, 1974), 628; Scott M. Huse, *The Collapse of Evolution* (Grand Rapids, MI: Baker Books, 1997).

4. Deane B. Judd and Günter Wyszecki, *Color in Business, Science and Industry—Wiley Series in Pure and Applied Optics*, third edition (New York: Wiley-Interscience, 1975), 388.

5. Howard Crosby Warren, *Human Psychology* (New York: Cornell University Library, 2009), 167.

6. Charles Darwin, *The Origin of Species: 150th Anniversary Edition* (New York: Penguin, 2003).

7. Lucille Keir, Barbara A. Wise, Connie Krebs, and Cathy Kelley-Arney, *Medical Assisting: Administrative and Clinical Competencies*, sixth edition (Australia: Cenage Learning, 2007), 377.

8. David G. Myers, *Psychology*, 4th edition (New York: Worth Publishers Inc, 1995), 43.

9. Tim LaHaye and David Noebel, *Mind Siege* (Nashville: Word Publishing, 2000), 45.

10. Scott Lafee, "Wellnews: All the News That's Fit," U-T San Diego, July 31, 2007, accessed December 17, 2015, http://www.utsandiego.com/uniontrib/20070731/news_lz1c31 wellnuz.html.

11. Sandra Aamodt and Sam Wang, *Welcome to Your Brain* (New York: Bloomsburg, 2008).

12. *Unlocking the Mystery of Life*, directed by Lad Allen (La Mirada, CA: Illustra Media, 2010), DVD.

13. Mark Eastman and Chuck Missler, *The Creator Beyond Time and Space* (Costa Mesa: CA: TWFT Publishers, 1996), 84.

### Chapter 2
### Ask for Directions

1. Daniel Kolenda, *Your Kingdom Come* (Orlando, FL: E-R Productions, 2011), 36–39.

### Chapter 3
### Give God a Vocabulary to Speak to You

1. Teresa Seputis, *How to Hear the Voice of God in a Noisy World* (Lake Mary, FL: Charisma House, 2001), 25–28.

### Chapter 4
### Learn How to Listen

1. C. R. Lovell, *Plants and the Skin* (Oxford: Blackwell Scientific Publications, 1993).

2. François Fénelon, *The Seeking Heart*, as quoted by Fred Smith in "Leader's Insight: How Integrity Grows," *Leadership Journal*, October 15, 2007.

## CHAPTER 5
### SEEK GOD'S KINGDOM FIRST

1. Paul Lee Tan, *Encyclopedia of 7700 Illustrations* (Rockville, Maryland: Assurance Publishers, 1984), 1208.

2. "Nate Saint," Mission Aviation Fellowship, accessed December 22, 2015, http://www.maf.org/about/history/nate -saint#.UDTsDKllRqM.

3. Kendra Cherry, "Hierarchy of Needs: The Five Levels of Maslow's Hierarchy of Needs," accessed December 22, 2015, http://psychology.about.com/od/theoriesofpersonality/a /hierarchyneeds.htm.

## CHAPTER 6
### SURRENDER YOUR WILL

1. A. W. Tozer, *The Pursuit of God* (Radford, VA: Wilder Publications, LLC, 2008), 21.

2. *The Very Best of Winds of Worship* (Double CD), copyright © 1998 Vineyard Music Group, "More Love, More Power" is dedicated to the memory of John Wimber (1934–1997), accessed December 22, 2015, http:// www.worship.co.za/series /mla-01.asp.

## CHAPTER 7
### TAKE ACTION!

1. Jack Canfield, *The Success Principles* (New York: Harper Collins Publishers, 2005), 102–103.

## CHAPTER 9
### DON'T LOSE FOCUS

1. John Maxwell, *Leadership Gold: Lessons Learned From a Lifetime of Leading* (Nashville, TN: Thomas Nelson, 2008).

2. R. Alec Mackenzie, *The Time Trap* (New York: McGraw-Hill Book Company, 1975).

3. As quoted by John Marks Templeton in *Worldwide Laws of Life: 200 Eternal Spiritual Principles* (Radnor, PA: Templeton Foundation Press, 1997).

4. Louis Pasteur quotes, ThinkExist.com, accessed December 22, 2015, http://thinkexist.com/quotes/louis _pasteur/.